MINIMUM WAGE

BOOK ONE: FOCUS ON THE STRANGE

by Bob Fingerman

Also by Bob Fingerman

White Like She
You Deserved It
Recess Pieces
Bottomfeeder
Connective Tissue
From the Ashes
Pariah
Maximum Minimum Wage

IMAGE COMICS, INC.
Robert Kirkman – Chief Operating Officer
Erik Larsen – Chief Financial Officer
Todd McFarlane – President
Marc Silvestri – Chief Executive Officer
Jim Valentino – Vice-President

Eric Stephenson – Publisher
Ron Richards – Director of Business Development
Jennifer de Guzman – Director of Trade Book Sales
Kat Salazar – Director of PR & Marketing
Corey Murphy – Director of Retail Sales
Jeremy Sullivan – Director of Digital Sales
Emilio Bautista – Sales Assistant
Branwyn Bigglestone – Senior Accounts Manager
Emily Miller – Accounts Manager
Jessica Ambriz – Administrative Assistant
Tyler Shainline – Events Coordinator
David Brothers – Content Manager
Jonathan Chan – Production Manager
Drew Gill – Art Director
Meredith Wallace – Print Manager
Monica Garcia – Senior Production Artist
Jenna Savage – Production Artist
Addison Duke – Production Artist
Tricia Ramos – Production Assistant
IMAGECOMICS.COM

MINIMUM WAGE, BOOK ONE: FOCUS ON THE STRANGE. First printing. October 2014. Published by Image Comics, Inc. Office of publication: 2001 Center Street, Sixth Floor, Berkeley, CA 94704. Contains material originally published as Minimum Wage #1-6 by Image Comics. Printed in the USA. For information regarding the CPSIA on this printed material call: 203-595-3636 and provide reference #RICH–585455. For international rights, contact: foreignlicensing@imagecomics.com. ISBN: 978-1-63215-015-8.

FOREWORD

When Bob asked me to write this prologue, I was kind of surprised. Flattered? Absolutely. But mostly surprised. I'm someone known mostly for writing ***Burn Notice***, a TV show whose only connection to the world of comics is that it's got a comic-book-ish story about a hero who fights injustice, etc. You know… the kind of stuff that is not in ***Minimum Wage*** at all.

So I guess I'm writing this mainly because I'm a fan. Which leads to the real question: Why am I a fan? Why is anyone? I mean, ultimately ***Minimum Wage*** is just a chronicle of a regular guy in his 20s stumbling through life in New York. He broods about a failed relationship. He has some friends. He dates, or tries to. And that's kind of… it. When I try to tell my friends about ***Minimum Wage***, it seems to dissolve as I describe it: "It's about this guy, Rob, he's an artist, he… he's recently divorced… um… sometimes he lives with his mom. It's great. Really."

The more I've gotten into the books, though, the more I've realized that it's the fact that it's undefinable that makes it what it is. Comics may have begun with heroic ego-projection fantasies, but one of the things they do best is the exact opposite of that: the personal, idiosyncratic internal narrative. A great comic can do everything the great character novel does – more, in some ways, putting us both inside and outside the main character at the same time.

I think that's one of the reasons we find ***Minimum Wage*** so compelling. I daresay no medium has ever captured the experience of jerking off to internet porn in your mom's house with such precision and artistry. Rob's intensely subjective desire, self-loathing, and anxiety are all there on the page, while the art in the panel places us just outside the action, so we see it in all its pathetic humanity. If Proust were alive today, and writing for alt-comics, I think he'd be doing the same kind of thing.

The truth is, though, meta-critical media analysis aside, I read ***Minimum Wage*** for the characters – characters so deeply realized I sometimes forget that they aren't just people I know. Sylvia has invaded my inner life so thoroughly that she feels like she's my ex. I've become oddly attached to Rob's friendships, too. Where else but in the pages of ***Minimum Wage*** can you find a guy like Matt? He's a douchebag who you love in spite of and because of the fact that he's a douchebag. I don't know that guy… but I *know* that guy.

So thanks, Bob. Thanks for the books, and thanks for the chance to write this piece and think about them. Maybe now, when one of my friends asks me to describe ***Minimum Wage***, I'll actually have something to say.

Matt Nix
Los Angeles

This book is dedicated, as ever, to my wife, Michele, the love of my life.
I really hope Rob gets to meet *his* Michele someday.
It is also dedicated to my late friend, John Walsh, who I miss every day.
The world is poorer for his absence and certainly less funny.

SATURDAY, MAY 8TH, 2000. LIDO BEACH, LONG ISLAND.
I CAN'T BELIEVE I FORGOT MY FUCKING WALLET.
IT'S NO BIG, DUDESTER. I GOT YOU COVERED. YOU'RE MY BITCH TONIGHT. I'LL JUST EXPECT A HANDIE LATER.
IT'S NOT THAT. THEY WON'T LET ME IN WITHOUT PROPER I.D..
BUSH
ROB'S RIGHT. THEY'RE NOT GOING TO LET HIM IN.
THANKS FOR THAT, MAXIMILIAN. SERIOUS, THANKS FOR THAT.
SNICKER
COULD YOU NOT LOOK SO MISERABLE, ROB? CHILLAX.
WANT ME TO "CHILLAX"? FIRST STEP: DON'T SAY "CHILLAX".
FINE. DONE.

SO, I.D.?
I FORGOT IT AT HOME.
NOT GETTIN' IN, THEN. NEXT.
I'M NOT JUST GONNA WAIT IN THE CAR LIKE A DOG WHILE THESE--
YEAH, ACTUALLY YOU ARE.
GREAT. JUST GREAT. I'M ON THE WRONG SIDE OF TWENTY-FIVE. I'M JUST DIVORCED...
AND NOW THIS: BEING KEPT OUT OF A PLACE I DON'T EVEN WANNA BE BECAUSE I--
NEVER MIND, GUY. JESUS, JUST GO IN.
WHAT?!?
(JUST GO IN, MAN. BUT DON'T ORDER FROM THE BAR OR I'LL LOSE MY JOB.)
SERIOUSLY? THAT'S TOTALLY DECENT OF--
JUST GO!
NEXT. LET'S SEE SOME I.D.
THAT WAS SOME STRAIGHT-UP JEDI MIND SHIT, BRONUS.
YOU JUST CAN'T FAKE THAT KIND OF BITTERNESS.
SAD, BUT TRUE.

YUP. AND SO IT GOES.
THERE'S THE PUNIM I HATE: THE "ROB SOURMASH." EXTRACT THE BUTTPLUG, KOBBA AND LIVE A LITTLE.
"KOBBA"?
MY SPECIAL NAME FOR A SPECIAL BOY.
YOU ARE SO THE 'MO FOR ROB IT MAKES ME SQUIRMY.
SQUIRMY AS IN JEALOUS THAT YOU'RE NOT MY SPECIAL BOY? DON'T BE JEALOUS, JEALOUS.
UGH, PLEASE. YOUR "SPECIAL BOY" NEEDS TO LEARN TO RELAX. YOU NEED A DRINK, "SPECIAL BOY." YOU LOOK DRY.
I AM DRY, BUT NOT FOR ALCOHOL. ALL THESE GYRATING GIRLS. IT'S BEEN AGES SINCE I'VE, UH--
PLANTED THE FLAG.
EXACTLY.
LAVENDER PARISOL
SO APPLY SOME CONVERSATIONAL LUBRICATION. I'M BUYING. THE USZH?
YEAH, I'LL HAVE A WHITE RUSSIAN.
THAT'S ADORABLE. SPECIAL BOY'S SPECIAL DRINK, SO HE CAN CATCH THE COURTESY VAN TO PUSSY TOWN. JUST DON'T ORDER A MUDSLIDE. I'VE BEEN RELIABLY INFORMED THAT'S A GIRL DRINK.
DULY NOTED.

YO! YO, BOSS! LEMME GET THREE VODKA RED BULLS!
HEY, CHIEF! STOLI RAZZ ON THE ROCKS AN' TWO MILLER LITES!
YO, GUY! SHOT A JAME-OH AN' A COORS LITE!
HOW DO YOU COMPETE WITH THAT?
BARKEEPS HATE GUYS LIKE THEM. BIG MOUTHS, SMALL TIPS. WATCH THE MASTER.
LAVENDER PARISOL
AHOY, GOODLY MIXOLOGIST! KINDLY SET UP THESE FINE-ASS WENCHES WITH THE LIBATIONS OF THEIR CHOOSING.
YOU FOR REAL, KID? LEMME SEE SOME I.D.
THIS PLACE HAS A REAL BONER FOR I.D.
THERE YOU GO, CHAMP! OH, AN' A GREY GOOSE GRAYHOUND, A WHITE RUSSIAN AN' WHAT'RE YOU HAVIN'?
A ROLLING ROCK.
UCCH. YOU SHAME ME.
AND WHAT'RE YOU TWO FINE PIECES OF MACKEREL CALLED? I'M MATT.
I'M TONI.
I'M TINA.
TONY AND TINA? LIKE THAT THEATER THING WHERE YOU TRAIPSE AROUND AS PART OF THE SHOW?
VENDE

OMIGAWD, WE GET THAT AWL TH' TIME! IT'S TOTALLY MENTAL!
YEAH, IT'S TOTALLY CRAZY!
LOCAL GIRLS, I TAKE IT?
BAWN AN' BRED, SOUTH SHAW.
MASSAPEQUA. TOTALLY.
WELL, ENJOY YOUR DRINKS, LADIES.
WOW, HE JUST BAWT US DRINKS AN' DIDN' HIT ON US. THAT'S CLASSY.
I KNOW, RIGHT? WE SHOULD TOTALLY BLOW HIM LATUH.
ROLL A
YOU CRAZY? YOU HAD THOSE TWO MAD TEED UP.
I CAME TO SEE THE BAND. THOSE TWO? UCCH. THEIR VOICES WERE PURE BONERCIDE. I CAN'T ROLL WITH THE LAWN GUYLAND ACCENT.
WHAT A FUCKING SNOB, YOU ARE. I'M FROM ROCK-AWAY. HOW'D I PASS YOUR STANDARDS TEST?
AND YOU'RE DRINKING A ROCK. I HAVE NO IDEA. BUT I'M NOT LOOKING TO BONE YOU.
NO, JUST ROB. THAT'S WHY YOU DIDN'T WANNA MAKE TIME WITH THOSE TWO HOTTIES.
RIGHT. HEY, IF THEY'RE ALL TEED UP, YOU GO TALK TO THEM, CASANOVA. MAKE THEIR VICTORIAS A LITTLE LESS SECRET.
THE MOMENT'S PASSED. YOU BLEW IT FOR US.
KEEP TELLING YOURSELF THAT, PEACHES.

WHY DID I COME? I DON'T LIKE THIS BAND. I HATE CLUBS. I'VE GOT ZERO CHANCE OF HOOKING UP. SORRY. I'M A WET BLANKET.
S'OKAY.
YO, YOUR CAUCASIAN.
NO ONE CALLS THEM THAT IN REAL LIFE. THAT'S LEBOWSKI'S, SOLAMENTE.
BITCH MOVES TO REGO PARK, SUDDENLY HE'S SENOR BILINGUO.
IF THE NABE AFFECTED ME THAT WAY IT'D BE UZBEK OR SOMESUCH.
DRINK, DRINK. LESS TALK, MORE DRINK. I WANNA SEE KOBS BUCK WILD, SLURRING AND SHIT.
CLINK
LOVE
HE JUST WANTS TO GET YOU TIPSY SO HE CAN HAVE HIS WAY WITH YOU.
OH, PLEASE. SERIOUS, DAWG, METHINKS IT IS YE PICTURING US DOING THE DASTARDLY A LA TOM O' FINLANDIA.
WHATEVER. BAND'S COMING ON.
THAT'S WHAT I'M TALKING ABOUT: DRINK, DRINK! I'LL GET YOU ANOTHER.
I INSIST. KOBBA'S GETTIN' LIT TONIGHT.
TONIGHT, TONIGHT, WON'T BE JUST ANY NIIIIGHT...
LAVENDER PARISOL

NOW MAX PUT THAT IMAGE IN MY HEAD.
YOU ACTUALLY DIVORCED YET?
STILL WAITING ON THE PAPERWORK. YOU CAN'T DO UNCONTESTED, SO WE WENT WITH ADULTERY.
HERS OR YOURS?
HERS.
DID SHE?
I'M NOT SURE. SHE WAS SPENDING A LOT OF TIME WITH--
APPEARING FOR THE FIRST TIME IN LONG ISLAND, BRING THE NOISE FOR LAVENDER PARISOL!
I'M GOING TO GO--
YEAH, NO SWEAT.
UGH. THIS IS TRULY LIMP-DICK MUSIC.
THE YARDS OF CLEAVAGE ARE DOING MY HEAD IN.
WHERE'S MATT WITH MY DRINK? FUCK IT, HE CAN HAVE IT.
SO, HERE WE ARE, AGAIN.
I'D RATHER BE OUT HERE, AFTER ALL. THAT BAND KIND OF BLOWS.
NOT A FAN OF THAT NEW WAVE CRAP. SLAYER, BABY. SLAY-ER.
DEFINITELY. HEY, THANKS FOR BEING DECENT BEFORE.
RANGERS

I CAN **SMELL** YOU GOT A DRINK OR TWO IN YA, BUT FUCK IT.

YOU **REALLY** DIVORCED?

YEAH, PRETTY MUCH. WAITING ON THE FINAL PAPERWORK.

THA'S PRETTY WACK. GOT MARRIED CRAZY YOUNG, HUH?

YEAH, I GUESS. TWENTY-TWO.

JEESH. SHE PREGNANT?

NAH. JUST... *STUFF*. IT HAPPENED. PREGNANT IS DEFINITELY WHAT SHE **WANTED** TO BE, THOUGH.

AN' YOU, NOT SO MUCH, ANH?

VERY NOT SO MUCH, NO. NO ROOM FOR COMPROMISE THERE, EITHER.

I GOT **TWO** KIDS AN' THEY'RE A HAN'FUL. AN' THEIR **MOTHER**? *PFFF.*

SO, HERE WE ARE.

JUST TH' WAY I LIKE IT. S'PEACEFUL.

IT'S NOT SO BAD, ACTUALLY.

2:25 A.M.
I DON'T MEAN TO TEASE SO MUCH ABOUT YOU AND MATT. IT'S JUST--
S'OKAY. BESIDES, MATT GOT HIS WISH TO DRIBBLE SOME FLUIDS ON ME.
EW, HE DROOLED ON YOU BACK THERE?
YUP. HE'S A SOUND SLEEPER. ANYWAY, THIS IS WHERE I GET OUT.
GUESS YOU'RE STUCK WITH MATT FOR THE NIGHT. SIX KETEL ONES, OR WHATEVER THE FUCK HE WAS DUMPING DOWN HIS GULLET. UGH.
IF YOU DO LEAVE HIM IN THE CAR, CRACK A WINDOW.
I'LL THINK ABOUT IT.
ANYWAY, SEEYA SOON, NEIGHBOR!
"NEIGHBOR." SIGH
BACK IN REGO PARK.
TOYOTA
BACK TO WHERE IT ALL BEGAN. THE MORE THINGS CHANGE... ONLY THIS IS PRETTY MAJOR. I DON'T EVEN HAVE MY OLD ROOM.
NOT THAT I SHOULD. NICE ENOUGH MOM'S ACCOMMODATING THIS SETBACK. MEANWHILE, SYLV IS SET UP IN A NEW APARTMENT, SWEET AS YOU PLEASE. FUCK.

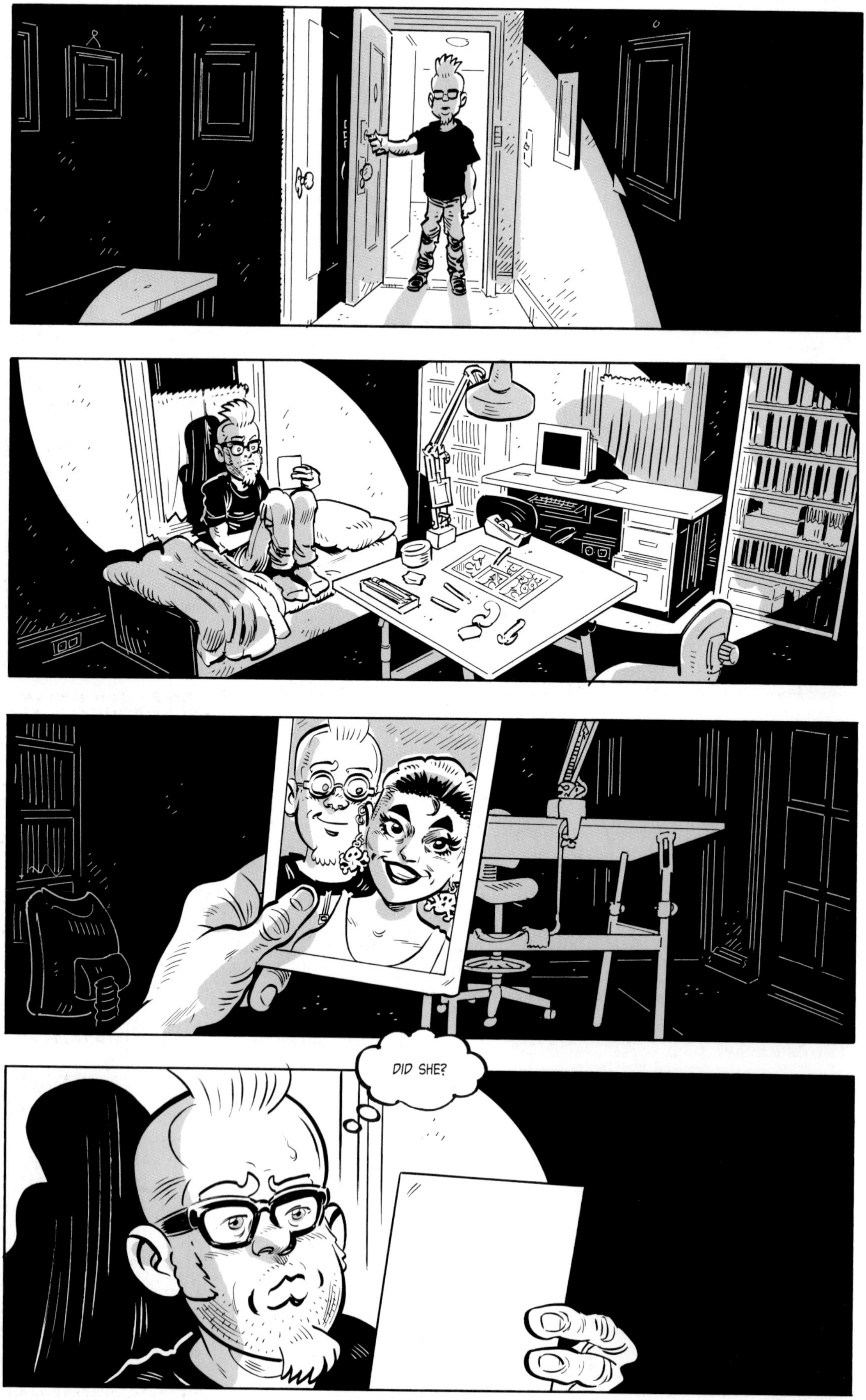

DID SHE?

MONDAY, MAY 10TH, NOON.
...DON'T KNOW IF WE SHOULD ACCEPT THOSE ZUCCHINI PILLOWS, GUYS.
OH, DON'T BE SO SUSPICIOUS. SEND THOSE BABIES UP, WE'LL USE 'EM IN THE RUMPUS ROOM.
THIS IS BLOWFUL. EVEN A MYSTIE MORNING ISN'T DOING IT FOR ME.
GOTTA GO. I GOTTA TURN IN MY LATEST FILTH. ≥SIGH≤
HOW SAD IS IT THAT I THINK SIGHS, TOO.
≥SIGH≤
CLIK!
"...'Can-D is obsolete, because what does it do? Provides a few moments of escape, nothing but fantasy. Who wants it? Who needs that when they can get the genuine thing from me?' He added."
Rego Park
63RD DRIVE
63RD DRIVE
NEW YORK KNICKS
PHILIP K. DICK
THE THREE STIGMATA OF PALMER ELDRITCH
ALTERNATE REALITIES DON'T SOUND SO BAD. I THINK I'D RATHER LIVE IN DICK'S SHITTY REALITY THAN THIS ONE.
CHRIST, THE R SUCKS. IT SUCKED IN BAY RIDGE AND IT SUCKS IN REGO PARK. ONE END OF THE LINE TO THE OTHER IT SUCKS.
OH, HERE WE GO. FINALLY.
63RD DRIVE
63 Drive
SHIT.
PHILIP K

SIGN THE PEH-TISH-UN! SIGN THE PEH-TISH-UN!
WOW, SHE'S STILL AT IT AFTER ALL THESE YEARS. I WONDER IF HER ANTI-PORN SPIDER-SENSE TINGLES WHENEVER I WALK BY.
STOP PORN!
X-PO
PORN DEGRADES EVERYONE
UPS
THE MORE THINGS CHANGE...
STILL, NICER OFFICES AND MUCH BETTER PAGE RATES THAN PORK. BUT STILL CHURNING OUT THE SNIZ 'TOONS. UGH.
SECOND AVENUE
HA! NICE. SO MUCH WORK FOR PAGES OUR "READERS" SKIP.
MEANING?
YOU THINK GANDER'S GONNA KEEP SHELLING OUT FOR NICETIES LIKE FUNNIES FOR MUCH LONGER? THIS INDUSTRY IS IN THE CRAPPER, MY FRIEND.
PAY DAVE
BUT PEOPLE LOVE PORN.
WHEN'S THE LAST TIME YOU PULLED YOUR PUD TO INK ON PAPER? IT'S ALL ABOUT THE PIXELS, KIDDO.
JESUS, WITHOUT THESE MAGS I'D BE IN TROUBLE DEEP.
WE'RE DINOSAURS HERE. I'M ALREADY--
(I'M ALREADY SCOPING OUT MY NEXT PORT OF CALL.) SHH.
JUNE
DEC

WHAT'RE YOU GENTS GASSING ABOUT?
THE ILL WIND OF CHANGE.
AH. THE DOOM THAT CAME TO SARNATH.
NOT EVERYTHING CAN BE A LOVECRAFT REFERENCE. WE MEAN WEB PORN.
ART
JAN - APR. SALES
32%
THAT'S WHERE YOU'RE WRONG. THE PEOPLES OF THRAA, ILARNEK, AND KADATHERON ARE THE WEB PORN SITES. WE ARE THE NATIVE MOON PEOPLE WHOSE DOMAIN IS BEING USURPED.
WE ARE THE DYING PRIESTS OF SARNATH AND IN BLOOD WE SCRAWL "DOOM."
MM, I DUNNO. BUT DOOM DOES LOOM.
AND THIS IS WHY I DRINK.
29%
29%
31%
35%
GIMME A SWIG, BOLESLAW.
THIS IS ALL VERY DISTRESSING. I AM DISTRESSED.
IT'S NOT AS BAD AS ALL THAT. BUT IT'S COMING. MAYBE NOT TODAY, MAYBE NOT TOMORROW...
BUT IT'S COMING.
IN THE MEANTIME, KEEP DRAWING US THEM BIG JUG TITTIES, SATCH.
IT'S WHAT I DO. BUT I GOTTA BRANCH OUT. NOW.
GO DRAW DONG FOR THE GAY MAGS WE PUBLISH. I MEAN THE MAGS FOR WOMEN... THAT ARE ONLY READ BY GAY DUDES.
THAT IS SO NOT WHAT I MEANT.

IS ROB GOING TO **FINALLY** DRAW SOME **WANG** FOR ME?
OH, HEY SHEILA. I DON'T THINK SO.
WHY NOT? IT'S NOT LIKE YOU DON'T DRAW **WEENIS** FOR ***SAMMY*** HERE.
YEAH, BUT FOR **ME** IT'S ***INCIDENTAL WEENIS.***

ACTUALLY, I THINK I USE'TA PLAY **DRUMS** FOR **INCIDENTAL WEENIS**.
CUTE.
MAYBE I SHOULD ASK SHEILA OUT. SHE'S NICE ENOUGH AND AT LEAST SHE'S NOT GUN-SHY ABOUT SEX.
BUT IF SHE **WASN'T** INTERESTED IT WOULD MAKE COMING HERE **AWKWARD**. CAN'T HAVE **THAT**. I NEED GANDER'S GOLDEN EGGS.
GODDAMMIT.

OKAY, CONFAB ADJOURNED. GET CRANKIN' ON ANOTHER PORNY PUN-FILLED TWO-PAGER, HOFFENFOFFER.
OUR READERS DEMAND THE VERY BEST.
I THOUGHT THEY **SKIP** THE COMICS.
THEY **DO**. JUST TRYING TO KEEP YOUR **MORALE** UP.
LONG AS THE **CHECKS** CLEAR MY MORALE IS JUST FINE.

SERIOUSLY, THOUGH: DOOM, MY FRIEND. WRIT LARGE. **DOOM.**

...SAMMY AND BOLESLAW SAID MADE ME NERVOUS.
THESE ARE NERVOUS TIMES, BUDDY. OUR DAYS ARE NUMBERED. MAYBE IT'S FOR THE BEST.
TOWER DINER
TOWER DINER
ONE WAY
THIS JOB I'M DOING IS PRETTY MUCH KILLING ME.
IT'S A CHERRY GIG, JACK. THE COVER FOR THE 40TH ANNIVERSARY ISSUE? THAT'S A BIG DEAL.
AND IT'S A FOUR-LEAF GATEFOLD. THEY'VE NEVER DONE ONE OF THOSE BEFORE.
HAS ANYONE? IT'S A BIG DEAL. FOR BIG PAY. BIG BIG TASTE IN A BIG BIG BITE.
YEAH. BUT IT'S STILL A LOT OF WORK.
BOO-HOO. IT'S PRESTIGIOUS AND I'M STILL GRINDING OUT SMUT.
BUT YOU'RE ALSO FINALLY DOING COMICS FOR SCREAMING METAL. THAT'S BIG.
TRUE. AND SOMEDAY I'LL GRADUATE TO MY OWN TITLE. THEN I'LL START THE INEVITABLE NAVEL-GAZING, DO SOMETHING QUASI-AUTOBIOGRAPHICAL AND THE SNAKE WILL DEVOUR ITS OWN TAIL.
OUROBOROS.
IF THAT'S THE SNAKE EATING ITS OWN TAIL.
IT IS.
AND YOU'LL FEATURE YOUR THINLY VEILED CHARACTER TALKING TO MY THINLY VEILED CHARACTER AND IT'LL BE SELF-REFERENTIAL AND META AND VERY HIP.
CHRIST, I HOPE NOT.
THIS BURGER'S GOOD.
NOTHING BEATS A GOOD DINER BURGER.
EXCEPT FUR BURGER.

EXCEPT THESE DAYS FUR BURGERS ARE FURLESS. JUST HOW I LIKE 'EM.
I REMEMBER WHEN YOU WERE WITH CARLA, BACK AT S.V.A. AND YOU DREW A NOT-SO-CRYPTIC LITTLE DIAGRAM FOR ME...
RESTROOMS
...LIKE THIS. RING ANY HAIRLESS BELLS?
HA! YEAH, I SAID I LIKED IT AND SHE DID IT FOR ME. BALD WASN'T AS COMMON THEN AS IT IS NOW.
OR SO I HEAR.
THE GOLDEN AGE OF SMOOTH MONS VENERIS.
SIGH I MIGHT TRY ONLINE DATING.
I SHOULD DO THAT, TOO. MUST BE WEIRD BEING SINGLE AGAIN.
WEIRD IS A WORD. YEAH, LET'S GO WITH WEIRD. SIGH

1:15 A.M.
I GOTTA GET A GIRL. AND AN APARTMENT. CHRIST, THE MORE THINGS CHANGE. I WAS STILL LIVING AT HOME WHEN SYLVIA AND I MET.
NOW I'M LOOKING TO MEET A NEW GIRL AND I'M BACK AT HOME WHILE I GET MY FINANCES BACK UP TO SNUFF.
2:20 A.M.
IT'S COOL THAT MOM'S LETTING ME CAMP HERE, BUT EMPTY NEST'S ARE SUPPOSED TO STAY EMPTY. AND IT FEELS WEIRD HERE, NOW. THE PORNY WORK I DO... IT FEELS EVEN MORE GROSS UNDER HER ROOF.
AND NOW THE SPECTER OF DATING. ONE PROFILE AFTER ANOTHER. IT'S A SMORGASBORD OF LONELINESS. I'D BETTER WRITE MINE.
3:18 A.M.
"SWM, 25, CARTOONIST/PORNOGRAPHER, SEEKS..." NO, THAT'S AWFUL. DON'T INCLUDE PORNOGRAPHER. BUT MAYBE I SHOULD. MAYBE THAT'D GET ME SOME FREE-SPIRITED... FREAK. IT WOULD GET ME A FREAK. THE WRONG KIND OF FREAK.
"SWM, 25, CARTOONIST, RECENTLY DIVORCED..." AM I INSANE? DON'T PUT THAT IN THERE.
4:00 A.M.
"SWM, 25, CARTOONIST..." C'MON, GUY, YOU'RE A WRITER, TOO. WRITE SOMETHING. "SWM, 25, CARTOONIST, BROKEN BY LIFE. WILLING TO END A MARRIAGE TO AVOID BREEDING..."
YEAH, THAT'S THE STUFF. LET'S FIND SOMEONE REALLY BITTER.
"HI, I'M ROB. I MAKE FUNNY PICTURES AND LIVE WITH MOMMY WHILE I LICK MY WOUNDS. LOOKING FOR SOMEONE TO LICK THEM WITH ME." PERFECT. KILL ME.
WHY IS THIS SO DIFFICULT? UH, BECAUSE MY SELF-ESTEEM IS AT AN ALL-TIME LOW? BUT I'M STILL A GOOD DUDE. UGH. UGH, UGH, UGH. OKAY, ONE MORE TRY...

NEXT DAY, NOONISH.
SLURP
IT'S LIKE MOM ISN'T EVEN HERE, OUR SCHEDULES ARE SO DIFFERENT. ANYWAY. OKAY. SPAM, SPAM, SPAM, SPAM...
IT'S LIKE AN UNFUNNY VERSION OF THAT PYTHON SKETCH.
MORE SPAM. WAIT: THAT'S NOT SPAM, THAT'S FROM THE DATING SITE.
AKIRA 4
AKIRA 5
AKIRA 6
TWENTY-FOUR PEOPLE CHECKED OUT MY PROFILE? SIX ACTUAL REPLIES? SIX?!?
I BARELY REMEMBER WHAT I WROTE BUT IT MUST'VE BEEN REALLY GOOD.
HUH. THEY DON'T LOOK LIKE MUTANTS AT FIRST BLUSH.
ACTUALLY, THREE OF THEM LOOK PRETTY PROMISING. MAYBE EVEN FOUR.
"CLVR-HANDL". HOPEFULLY THAT'S CLEVER HANDLE, NOT CLEAVER HANDLE. OKAY, SHE'S A LITTLE OLDER, BLONDE, ACTRESS/MUSICIAN. HMM. NO, NO, THAT'S FINE.
DATING
LOOK AT YOU, BACK ON THE HORSE. YOU'RE DEFINITELY GOING TO NEED YOUR OWN PLACE AGAIN. AND SOON.
LOTS OF PEOPLE LIVE AT HOME LONGER IN THIS ECONOMY. BUT YOU'RE RIGHT.
I'VE HAD OKAY LUCK WITH THE ONLINE STUFF. SORT OF. SOMETIMES. ANYWAY, GLAD YOU TOOK MY ADVICE.
DID I? OKAY.

GONNA BE STRANGE FOR YOU TO GET WITH SOME STRANGE AFTER, UM...
VERY. YOU CAN SAY THE NAME, MAX.
SYLVIA. YOU REALLY DON'T WANT KIDS, DO YOU?
NOPE. THERE WAS MORE TO IT THAN THAT, BUT NOTHING I CARE TO TALK ABOUT. GOTTA FOCUS ON THE STRANGE.
I LIKE THAT. SOUNDS VERY ZEN.
WAIT, WHY'D YOU GET QUIET? WHERE'D THE ZEN GO?
YOU SAID HER NAME.
WHUH-- YOU SAID IT WAS OKAY TO SAY HER NAME! I WASN'T GOING TO SAY IT BUT YOU SAID--
NOT YOUR FAULT.
IT'S A PROCESS. LEARNING TO BE WITHOUT SOMEONE I SHOULDN'T HAVE BEEN WITH IN THE FIRST PLACE.
BUT IT WASN'T ALL BAD, RIGHT?
NO. NO, I DON'T WANNA GIVE THAT IMPRESSION. I HAVE NO AXE TO GRIND. IT'S JUST-- SIGH
AND THINGS GET VULNERABLE AND I HAVE TO BE A DICK AND LEAVE. I HAVE A MEETING AT--
S'OKAY, GO. GLAD WE COULD GRAB A QUICK BITE. SEE YOU LATER, MAYBE, IN THE 'HOOD?
IT'S WEIRD HAVING YOU JUST A FEW BLOCKS AWAY. BUT YEAH, MAYBE. YOU'LL BE FINE. FOCUS ON THE STRANGE.
I'LL DO THAT.

≷SNIFF≶
FUCK.
"FOCUS ON THE STRANGE." ONWARD.
IT'S NICE TO ACTUALLY HAVE A MEAL WITH MY SON. HAVING YOU HERE HAS FELT MORE LIKE NOT HAVING YOU HERE.
FOR ME IT'S BEEN LIKE YOU'RE ONE OF THE UNSEEN ADULTS IN PEANUTS.
MWAH-MWUH-WAH-WAH-WUH.
HA! EXACTLY. I MISSED YOUR MEATBALLS AND SPAGHETTI.
FUNNY, CONSIDERING YOU WERE MARRIED TO AN ITALIAN.
I KNOW. ≷SIGH≶
I SHOULDN'T HAVE SAID THAT.
IT'S OKAY. I CAN'T SHUT DOWN EVERY TIME SHE COMES UP. ANYWAY, I'M TRYING ONLINE DATING.
SO SOON?
NO TIME LIKE THE PRESENT. I'M LONELY.
LONELY? YOU HAVE YOUR FRIENDS A FEW BLOCKS AWAY.
LONELY IS MY POLITE WAY OF MEANING SOMETHING ELSE, MA.
OH? OH. GOTCHA.

AND SO... MONDAY, MAY 15TH.
OKAY, FIFTEEN MINUTES LATE. OFF TO A ROCKY START. BUT SHE WAS THE FIRST TO AGREE TO MEET UP AND HER PROFILE LOOKED PROMISING.
IS THAT HER? NO. NOT UNLESS SHE'S... NO, THAT'S NOT HER. IT WOULD BE AMAZING TO GET STOOD UP RIGHT OUT OF THE GATE.
TARBUCKS
MAGAZINES
BUT WE'RE DOING THE WHOLE "SAFE" THING: PUBLIC PLACE, LUNCHTIME, MIDTOWN. AND I WAS HONEST IN MY PROFILE.
THOUGH I DID LEAVE OUT THE DIVORCE THING. SIN OF OMISSION?
ARE YOU ROBERT?
HUH? OH, YEAH, UM, ROB. YEAH.
SORRY, SORRY. ROB. I'M NATALIE.
YEAH, YES, OF COURSE. HI.
SORRY I'M LATE. I COULDN'T GET AWAY. NEW PRODUCT DAY.
OKAY, SO SHE'S NOT BAD LOOKING. NOT AS GOOD AS-- SHUT UP. JUST BE HAPPY SHE SHOWED.
CAN I HELP YOU?
UH YEAH: GRANDE CINNAMON DOLCE LATTE AND--

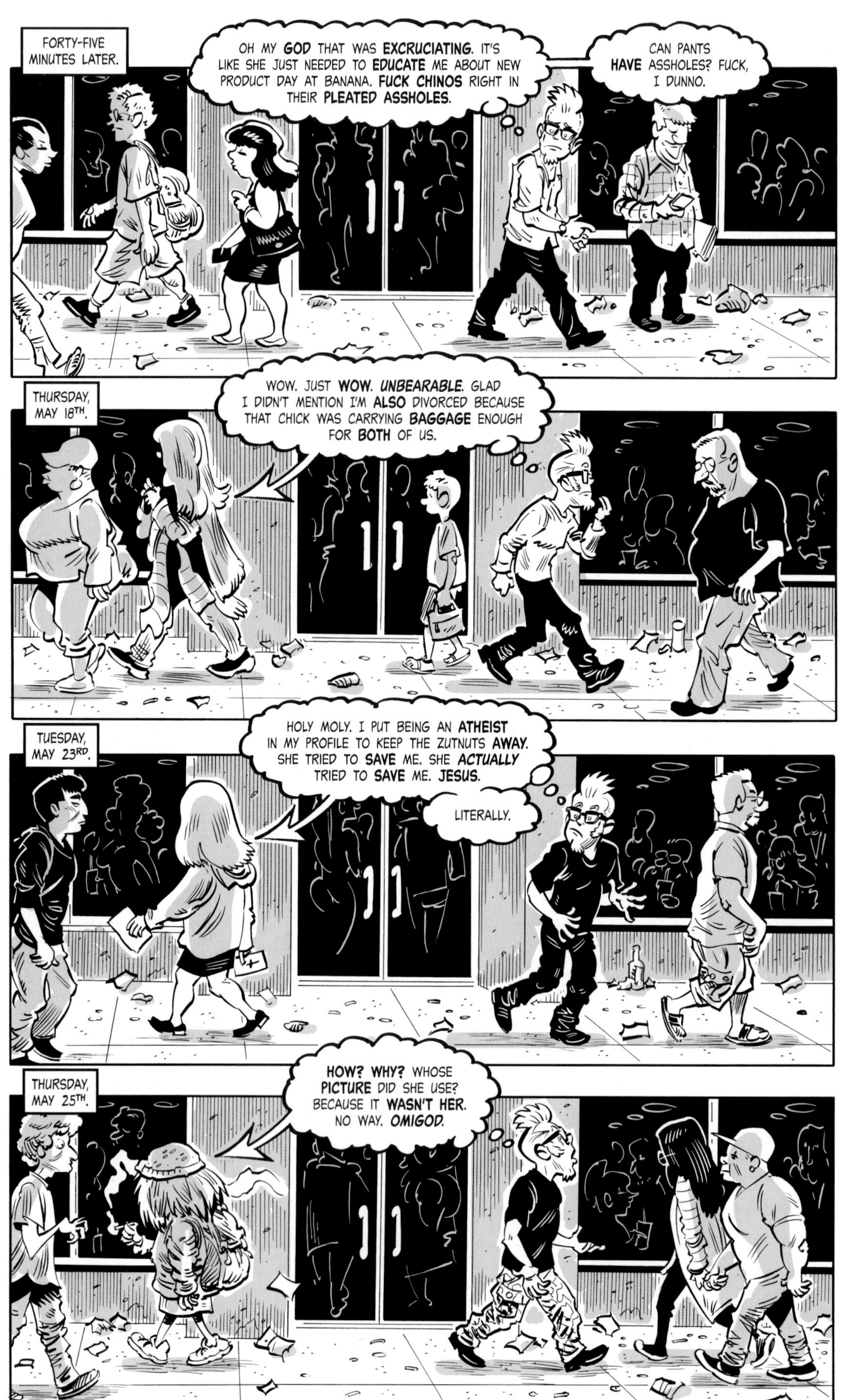
FORTY-FIVE MINUTES LATER.
OH MY GOD THAT WAS EXCRUCIATING. IT'S LIKE SHE JUST NEEDED TO EDUCATE ME ABOUT NEW PRODUCT DAY AT BANANA. FUCK CHINOS RIGHT IN THEIR PLEATED ASSHOLES.
CAN PANTS HAVE ASSHOLES? FUCK, I DUNNO.
THURSDAY, MAY 18TH.
WOW. JUST WOW. UNBEARABLE. GLAD I DIDN'T MENTION I'M ALSO DIVORCED BECAUSE THAT CHICK WAS CARRYING BAGGAGE ENOUGH FOR BOTH OF US.
TUESDAY, MAY 23RD.
HOLY MOLY. I PUT BEING AN ATHEIST IN MY PROFILE TO KEEP THE ZUTNUTS AWAY. SHE TRIED TO SAVE ME. SHE ACTUALLY TRIED TO SAVE ME. JESUS.
LITERALLY.
THURSDAY, MAY 25TH.
HOW? WHY? WHOSE PICTURE DID SHE USE? BECAUSE IT WASN'T HER. NO WAY. OMIGOD.

CLVR-HANDL FINALLY GOT BACK TO ME. IF HER ATTRIBUTES ARE REAL SHE MUST'VE HAD TO BEAT OFF DOZENS OF WANNABE SUITORS.
SO TO SPEAK.
SO TO THINK. WHOEVER IT WAS THAT SAID PEOPLE THINK MORE CONCEPTUALLY IN ELECTRIC IMPULSE SHORT-HAND AND NOT FULL SENTENCES NEVER MET ME.
I'M NERVOUS THIS TIME. THE OTHERS WERE DUDS, BUT I HAVE A GOOD FEELING ABOUT THIS ONE, WHICH GIVES ME A TERRIBLE FEELING.
AND IT'S NOT LIKE I'VE NEVER BEEN STOOD UP BEFORE. JEEZ, THAT TIME WAY BACK WHEN I WAS--
ROB?
STARBUCKS
COFFEE
HOLY SHIT: JACKPOT. DON'T BLOW IT. DO NOT BLOW IT.
MAY?
YES, HI. I'M MAY. YEAH. SORRY I'M LATE.
ARE YOU? YOU AREN'T. NOT AT ALL.
HEY, YOU MIND IF WE GO TO THE DINER AROUND THE CORNER? I KINDA HATE STARBUCKS.
JEEZ, I JUST REALIZED I PICKED THE RENDEZVOUS. IT'S PAVLOVIAN. I'M CONDITIONED TO MEET AT STARBUCKS.
BEEN ON A LOT OF THESE LATELY?
UH, I DON'T--
I'VE BEEN ON A LOT, TOO.
YOUR PROFILE ON S'LOVE IS VERY GOOD.
SO'S YOURS. DINER?

AN HOUR AND CHANGE LATER.
...GOT DIVORCED YOUNG. I WASN'T EVEN SURE I SHOULD MENTION IT, BUT GOSH, YOU TOO.
I KNOW, RIGHT? ME EITHER. I WAS LIKE, "TO TELL OR NOT TO TELL." AT LEAST ON A FIRST DATE.
IS THAT WHAT THIS IS: A DATE?
I DON'T KNOW. IS IT?
IT FEELS LIKE A DATE.
IT DOES, DOESN'T IT?
THE OTHERS HAVE FELT LIKE AUDITIONS FOR A PART I DIDN'T WANT. BUT NOT THIS ONE.
WOW.
YOU WANNA GET OUT OF HERE?
OKAY.
I'LL GET THE CHECK.
YOU MIND?
WHAT?
THE ARM. MY ARM. LIKE THIS.
NOT AT ALL. IT FEELS GOOD.
IT DOES, DOESN'T IT?
CHRIST, I HOPE SHE ISN'T AN AXE MURDERER. OR HAS A DICK. OR IS A REPUBLICAN. OR ALL THREE.
THIS IS A BIT FAMILIAR SO SOON. WAIT: WHAT?!? WHAT'RE YOU THINKING?!? ENJOY THIS. JESUS, ROB, YOU ARE A PIECE OF WORK.

MONDAY, JUNE 5TH.
LISTEN AGAIN. NO, LISTEN AGAIN. IT'S BRILLIANT.
BRIAN, ARE YOU STILL PLAYING THAT MESSAGE MY MOM LEFT? THAT'S SO NOT COOL.
SHUT UP AND WATCH YOUR PROGRAM, BUBELEH. IT IS BRILLIANT. LISTEN:
PRONG
MAX, THIS IS YOUR MOTHER. YOUR FRIENDS ARE MORONS, THEY REALLY ARE. WHAT IF ONE OF MY FRIENDS CALLS YOU? I'D BE SO EMBARRASSED.
AND WHY ARE YOU MORONS?
NOT YOU, WE. YOU'RE INCLUDED.
AH: THE OUT-GOING MESSAGE.
DING-DING-DING. GOLD STAR FOR ROBBY!
SNICKER
YOUR MOM DOESN'T THINK THE MESSAGE WE MADE IS FUNNY?
YOU MADE. YOU AND BRI'. NO, SHE DOESN'T THINK IT'S FUNNY.
YOUR MOTHER IS A LOVELY WOMAN, BUT SHE'S COMEDY ILLITERATE.
TRUE. ANYWAY, I'D BE WAY MORE EMBARRASSED IF ONE OF HER YENTA FRIENDS CALLED. FRANKLY, I'M AMAZED SHE HASN'T TOLD THEM TO.

HI, YOU'VE REACHED THE GOLDEN PORTAL ALL-MALE CINEMA. CURRENTLY SHOWING PORTER AT LARGE. "OH MY, THIS FLOOR IS ALL STICKY. SAAAAY, THAT'S QUITE A MOP HANDLE YOU'VE GOT THERE." BE SURE TO ASK ABOUT MEMBERSHIP TO OUR J.O. CLUB. LEAVE AN EMISSION AT THE-- BEEEP!
I DON'T HEAR ANYTHING AMISS.
YOU GUYS ARE MORONS.
OOH, NICE. ≷SQUACK≶
PRONG
I CAN'T BELIEVE YOU HAVE THE STONES TO GIVE US GRIEF, WHEN YOU MAKE THAT GROSS SOUND EVERY TIME SOME HOTTIE SHOWS UP ON SCREEN.
WHAT?!? WHAT ARE YOU EVEN TALKING ABOUT?
YOU'RE KIDDING, RIGHT? EVERY TIME A PAIR OF TITS COMES ON SCREEN YOU MAKE THIS JUICY ≷SQUACK≶ SOUND, LIKE AN INCONTINENT DUCK.
YOU'RE INSANE.
Corona
YOU DEFINITELY MAKE A SOUND, MAX.
IT'S TRUE. AND OH SO VERY SAD.
YOU GUYS ARE SO FULL OF SHIT.
PRONG
≷SQUACK≶
HE JUST-- I-- I MEAN--
IT'S LIKE TOURETTE'S. THE POOR SCHMO DOESN'T EVEN KNOW HE'S DOING IT. HE SEES BAGINA ON TEEVEE AND MOUTH-QUEEFS.
PRONG

SPEAKING OF, HOW'S IT GOING WITH THE NEW GIRL?
"SPEAKING OF"? IN WHAT WAY WERE WE--
DO NOT BE A DICK. SPILL.
I LIKE HER. YEAH. SHE'S NICE. VERY NICE.
PRONG
NICE. ⪢PFF⪡ KITTENS ARE NICE. BLAND THINGS ARE NICE.
YOU'RE NOT.
ZING. IS SHE NICE-NICE? LIKE, NICE?
NICE ENOUGH FOR YOU TO MAKE INVOLUNTARY QUEEF NOISE?
I DON'T DO--
FUCK YOU.
HEH-HEH.
PRONG
SO, WHEN YOU MOVING OUT OF YOUR MOM'S PLACE? YOU LOOKING AT ANYTHING YET?
S'MATTER, YOU DON'T LIKE HAVING ME SO CLOSE BY? MAYBE I'LL MOVE IN RIGHT NEXT DOOR.
PLEASE NO. KIDDING.
I STILL HAVE A LITTLE MENDING NEEDED, RE MY FINANCES. FEW MORE CHECKS AND I'LL START LOOKING. WHICH I DREAD. GOD... JUST BRUTAL.
WONDER IF I'LL HAVE TO PULL THAT SAME SCAM AS LAST TIME, PRETENDING TO WORK AT AN OFFICE.
PRONG
IF SO, I'LL USE GANDER THIS TIME.
IT'S A STEP UP FROM PORK, ANYWAY.
LATERAL MOVE, BUT THINGS AIN'T THE SAME AT PORK SINCE YOU LEFT.
GOD HELP THE POOR BASTARDS STILL WORKING UNDER SHEL, MAY HE DIE BADLY AND ROAST IN HELL.
I MARVEL AT THE DEPTHS OF YOUR HATRED.
YOU DIDN'T WORK FOR HIM.
PRAISE JESUS, NO.
PRONG
BREEP-BREEP!

HELLO? OH HI. YEAH. JUST HANGING WITH THE FELLAS. YEAH, OKAY. SEEYA SOON.
WAS THAT YOUR LADY? SHOULD I MAKE THE WHIP-CRACK SOUND?
BETTER THAT THAN THE PUSSY FART. HEY, WHAT CAN I SAY? I'M IN DEMAND.
FINE, BLOW US OFF FOR PUNANI. SEE IF WE CARE.
PRONG
"PUNANI." NOT YET. THAT'S GONNA BE WEIRD. MAY SEEMS LIKE A SWEET GIRL, BUT MAYBE A LITTLE RETICENT. BY THE SECOND OR THIRD DATE SYLV AND I WERE--
STOP IT. DON'T THINK ABOUT HER. YOU'RE DAYS FROM SIGNING DIVORCE PAPERS AND THEN YOU'RE FREE AND SHE CAN KNOCK OUT AS MANY BABIES AS--
SHUT THE FUCK UP, BRAIN. JUST SHUT THE FUCK UP. YOU'RE NOT HELPING.
WHAT? CAN'T A GUY ARGUE WITH HIS OWN BRAIN?
PFFF I SAY NOTINK.
PRONG
STRANGE HOW THIS NEIGHBORHOOD HAS CHANGED SINCE I WAS A KID. ALMOST ALL UZBEKISTANI NOW. MAKES ME THINK OF THAT SCTV BIT: "UZBEKS."
THAT'S IT: THINK ABOUT SCTV. THAT MAKES ME HAPPY.
НТА
Й СЕРВИС
ДАЁТСЯ
МЕСТО
В РЕНТ
ЕЛЕФОННЫЕ
АРТОЧКИ
В ПРОДАЖЕ ИМЕЮТСЯ
ГАЗЕТЫ И ЖУРНАЛЫ
ИЗ
РОССИИ И УКРАИНЫ

ROW HOUSES. I **HATED** LIVING IN THAT **HOUSE** AT THE END THERE. THE MOVE WAS PURE **POWER PLAY**. SYLV **DEMANDED** A ROOM OF HER OWN AND **NEVER** SET FOOT IN IT.
UH, YOU'RE DOING IT **AGAIN**, DICKHEAD. **SMOTHER** THE BAD THOUGHTS.
BZZZZT!
PRONG
I'M GLAD YOU WERE FREE. I NEEDED SOME COMPANY. WAS I INTERRUPTING--
NO, NO. JUST HANGIN' WITH MY BUDS. GETTING OUT OF MY MOM'S HAIR.
WOW, THAT SOUNDS LOSER-ISH. I--
NO, NO. YOU EXPLAINED ALREADY. **I** OWE MONEY. EVEN STREET-VENDING HANDMADE JEWELRY REQUIRES STARTUP CAPITAL. DRINK?
YEAH, ANYTHING. SODA, WATER--
IS SODA WATER TOO ON THE NOSE?
NO, PERFECT. WHAT'S THE MUSIC?
ALISON KRAUSS. DO YOU LIKE HER?
NOT FAMILIAR. KINDA COUNTRY.
YEAH. I'M GUESSING PRONG **ISN'T**.
NOT SO MUCH, NO.
. . DON'T
I THINK
VE YOU STA
S AND NIGHT
YOUR OWN
LONG AGO
PRONG

WANT ME TO CHANGE THE MUSIC? I CAN CHANGE THE MUSIC IF YOU DON'T--
NO, NO. IT'S FINE.
THIS IS LIKE WHEN I WAS **THIRTEEN**. I'M GETTING A **BONER** AND ***NOTHING*** IS HAPPENING. EXCEPT SEEING HER **ASS**. WHICH LOOKS INVITINGLY CUSHIONY.
BOY, THIS HITS THE SPOT. *GLUG-GLUG-GLUG*
PRONG
BOARRRP!
PRONG
OMIGOD, I AM **SO EMBARRASSED**. CLUB SODA MAKES ME... JEEZ, I AM...
SHHHH. JUST KISS ME.
YOU HAVEN'T SEEN MY BEDROOM YET.
I-- OKAY. NO, I HAVEN'T.
IS **THIS** HAPPENING? THIS **IS** HAPPENING. I DON'T HAVE CONDOMS. *DON'T GET AHEAD OF YOURSELF.* BUT THIS **IS** HAPPENING. **IS** THIS HAPPENING? IT IS. *IS IT?*
PRONG

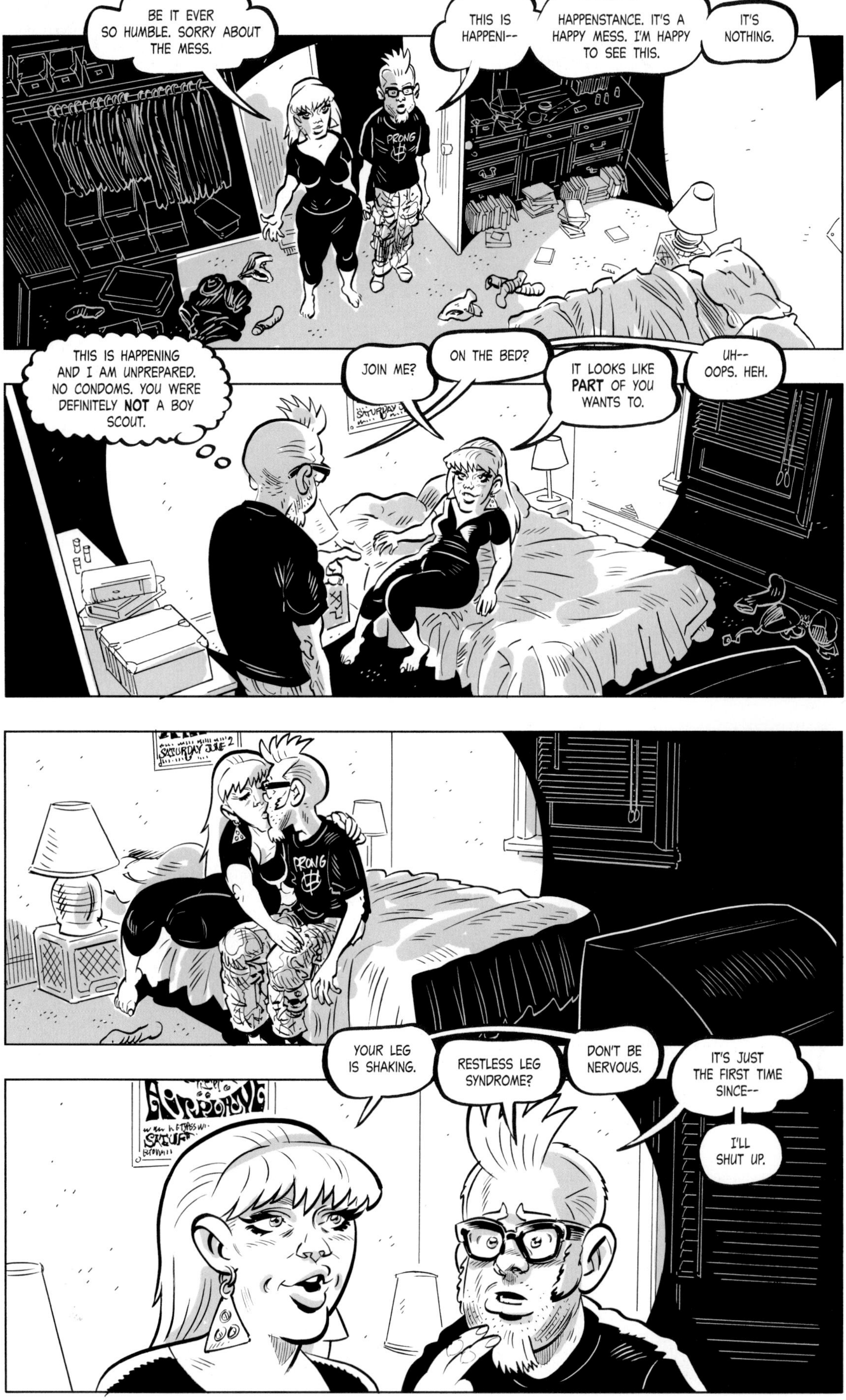

BE IT EVER SO HUMBLE. SORRY ABOUT THE MESS.

THIS IS HAPPENI--

HAPPENSTANCE. IT'S A HAPPY MESS. I'M HAPPY TO SEE THIS.

IT'S NOTHING.

THIS IS HAPPENING AND I AM UNPREPARED. NO CONDOMS. YOU WERE DEFINITELY **NOT** A BOY SCOUT.

JOIN ME?

ON THE BED?

IT LOOKS LIKE **PART** OF YOU WANTS TO.

UH-- OOPS. HEH.

YOUR LEG IS SHAKING.

RESTLESS LEG SYNDROME?

DON'T BE NERVOUS.

IT'S JUST THE FIRST TIME SINCE--

I'LL SHUT UP.

DAMN, I **REALLY** WANTED TO **SEE** HER BODY. I'M **ALL** ABOUT THE **VISUALS**. OKAY. GOTTA GO **BRAILLE**. OKAY, FINGERS: ***CREATE THE PICTURE***.

AND OTHER SENSES. HER **BREATH** IS REALLY WARM. SHE **SMELLS NICE**. SHE'S LETTING ME UNDRESS HER, ANYWAY. OKAY. **SHIRT'S OFF**. SMOOTH SKIN. OF **COURSE** IT IS. WHAT DID YOU EXPECT, **SCALES**?

POP-POP-POP---POP

NEVER WAS GOOD WITH **BRA HOOKS**. DON'T EMBARRASS ME, DIGITS. OKAY: **ONE HOOK UNDONE**. ANOTHER. ***THREE?*** WHOA, **FOUR HOOKS**. OFF. TAKE A BREATH. TAKE A DEEP BREATH. KEEP LIPS ENGAGED. **TONGUE**. NICE.

HAND ON BOOB. HAND IS **ON BOOB**. OKAY HAND, SEND THE PICTURE: **BUMPY AREOLA**. *NICE*, THOUGH. **LARGE NIPPLES**. GOD, HOW I WISH I COULD **SEE** WHAT'S HAPPENING.

CLINK

SHE'S UNDOING MY BELT. *OH JESUS.* YUP. IT'S UNDONE. SHE'S PULLING IT OUT OF THE LOOPS. ON THE FLOOR. **ZIPPER**. LIFT HIPS SO SHE CAN... ***OKAY, PANTS COMING OFF.***

KA-THUNK

BOTH PANTS OFF. UNDERPANTS STILL ON. OKAY, DIGITS, NEXT REPORT: ***FULL COVERAGE OR THONG?***

BZZZZZT

THONG. *YOU'RE* AN ARTIST: **PICTURE IT**. DON'T WANNA. I WANNA **SEE** IT. WITH AMBIENT LIGHT I **SHOULD** SEE **PLENTY**. *THIS IS THE CITY.* BUT **THIS** IS LIKE **COUNTRY DARK**. WHAT GIVES? ***STOP THINKING!***

IS THIS ALL RIGHT?

I-- YES. OF COURSE.

FIRST MOUTH ON ME SINCE--

DO **NOT** *FINISH THAT THOUGHT.*

SLURP-SLURP-SLURP

DOES SHE HAVE A **FULL-BACK SWASTIKA TATTOO** WITH "*PROPERTY OF THE ARYAN NATION*"? **SHUT UP, SHUT UP, SHU**---*HHH*-- OH **YEAH**, *THAT'S THE STUFF.* YES.

WEDNESDAY, JUNE 7TH.
IT'S SUCH A RELIEF THESE THINGS ARE OUT IN THE OPEN LIKE THIS NOW. IT WAS SUCH A HASSLE BACK IN THE DAY.
CONDOMS? THEY SUCK. MICRO-THIN, SUPER-SENSITIVE? BALONEY. I HATE THEM.
NOW OPEN! DR
NOW OPEN! DR
NOW OPEN! DR
NOW OPEN! DR
FIRST TIME I BOUGHT 'EM I WAS SO HUMILIATED I COULDN'T GET IT UP. ANYTHING GAVE ME WOOD BUT WHEN I GOT BACK INTO BED WITH KARRI, NOTHING.
I REMEMBER THAT. I MEAN, YOU TELLING ME ABOUT IT.
YOUR DRUGSTORE
SKYN
durex
WHAT EIGHTEEN-YEAR-OLD DOESN'T GET WOOD WHEN PRESENTED WITH VAGINA?
THE TRAUMATIZED KIND? BUT THEN YOU DID, AND--
IT SLIPPED OFF MID-FUCK. FIRST TIME I EVER USED ONE.
AND THEN SHE HAD TO FISH IT OUT. YOU AND SHE WERE VERY HAPPY WHEN AUNT FLO ARRIVED A FEW DAYS LATER.
I ALSO REMEMBER YOU SAYING IT HAD FINALLY BEGUN TO FEEL GOOD, OBVIOUSLY AFTER IT HAD SLIPPED OFF. FEH.
durex
K-Y INTENSE
ANYWAY, IF MAY AND I HAD HAD THESE WE'D HAVE TOTALLY DONE THE DEED.
YEAH. WEARING A WET-SUIT IN THE PITCH BLACK. NO THANKS.
SO YOU'D RATHER NO SEX THAN SEX IN THE DARK?
IF YOU CAN'T SEE IT, WHAT'S THE POINT?
YOU'LL FORGIVE ME FOR NOT WAITING ON LINE WITH YOU. I DON'T WANT ANYONE TO THINK THEY'RE FOR US.

EVEN FISHIES AT THE BOTTOM OF THE BRINY HAVE BIOLUMINESCENCE. THERE ARE FUNGI THAT GLOW. SEX IN THE DARK IS LIKE A TREE FALLING ALONE IN THE WOODS: IF NO ONE SAW IT, DID ANYONE COME?
YOU'RE MURDERING YOUR METAPHORS.
I THINK WE KNOW WHAT YOU MET HER FOR.
AND THE PUN. DIAGNOSIS: TOO MUCH BENNY HILL.
I GOTTA HEAD HOME. THE FOUR-LEAF GATEFOLD COVER AWAITS.
HOW MANY WEEKS HAVE YOU BEEN AT THAT?
TRY MONTHS. IT'S A LONG DEADLINE.
PARKINSON'S LAW: "WORK EXPANDS SO AS TO FILL THE TIME AVAILABLE FOR ITS COMPLETION."
ANYWAY. ASSUMING SHE'S VISIBLE, WHEN DO I GET TO MEET HER?
IT'S A LITTLE SOON.
WHATEVER, JEFE. SEE YOU LATER. SEE. NOT GROPE BLINDLY AT. SEE.
OKAY, OKAY. LATER, DUDE.
I WISH I DISAGREED. I REALLY DO. WHY ARE MEN SO HARDWIRED FOR VISUAL STIMULI?
I'D HAVE FELT SCARS, MOLES, FUR. SHE FELT NICE. I'M SURE SHE LOOKS NICE. I WANNA SEE! JACK IS RIGHT. I--
BREEP-BREEP!
YO, HOFBRAU, SUP? YOU FREE? I GOT A CRISIS AND I NEED MY MOST GROWN-UPPEST MATEY'S HELP.
REAL CRISIS OR MATT CRISIS?
I LIKE THAT. THAT'S MY SUPER-SECRET SPY NOM DE ESPIONAGE: CRISIS, MATT CRISIS. I'LL TAKE MINE SHAKEN AND STIRRED.
IS THERE AN ACTUAL CRISIS?
I LOVE IT. I CAN HEAR THE IMPATIENCE. YES. DUDE. A REAL ONE THAT REQUIRES YOUR EYES ONLY.
GODZILLA
AND SO...

A MODEL KIT. A FUCKING KAIJU MODEL KIT. AND I SHOULDN'T SLOWLY MURDER YOU WHY?
DUDE! DUDE? DUDE. CALMNESS. I SAID I NEED YOUR EYES. I HAVE NAE WEE GLASSES, LADDIE AND CANNOT SEE WHERE THE MISSING PIECES WENT. I FELT AROUND LIKE BLIND PEW. OH. FEELIN' AROUND.
OOF. THOSE ABS. IS KOBBA RIPPED? I BET YOU'RE RIPPED, SIX-PACK STYLIE. EIGHT-PACK. AM I RIGHT? LET'S GET NUDE AND WRESTLE.
JOSHING. ONLY. JUST FUCKIN' WITH KOBS TO GET A RISE. ANGER RISE, NOT BONE-YOBBA-PORK-SWORD RISE.
FUCK IT. WHATEV'S. I CAN BUY ANOTHER KIT IF YOU NO WANNA LOOK-SEE FOR THE MISSING PIECES.
GRAMPA KOBS! PLAYSTATION ONE. IT'S GONNA BE THE SHIT. WAIT. WAIT. WHAT IS THAT?!?
YO. I'M JONESING, BRO: PSONE DROPS IN JULY. AND I'M HAVING IT.
THE FUCK IS PEE ESS ONE?
IS THAT--? IS THAT A STUDDED METAL BRACELET?!?
IT IS! DUDE? DUDE. DUDE! OMIGOD, THAT'S ADORABLE.
I'M TAKING IT OFF.
NO WAY, BRONUS. IT'S AWESOME. IT'S 'EAVY, MAHN. 'EVVY MEH-UHL. BLEEDIN' 'EVVY, YEAH?
UGH. I DON'T EVEN. UHHH
NO, IT'S COOL. IT'S COOL. I LIKE ALL THE PARAPHERNALIA, YO. THE ROCKIN' TEE. LOOKIN' FORWARD TO SENIOR YEAR? THE PROM?
YOU MOCKING ME ABOUT IMMATURITY. THIS IS A NEW LOW. I DON'T GIVE YOU GRIEF OVER THE LIMP-WRISTED SHIT YOU LIKE.
IT'S OKAY TO LASH OUT. VERY METAL. THIS NEW PHASE--
NEW? I'VE LIKED METAL FOREVER.
YEAH, MAYBE. BUT YOU NEVER WORE IT ON YOUR SLEEVE. OR WRIST. OH, SNAPPA! SNOOSH! SWIRLY FOR THE SPORT-BALL SCORE.

TOUCHÉ.

THAT'S MY BOY. TAKIN' IT LIKE A MAN.

4:46 P.M.
GOD, THIS CONNECTION SUCKS. HOW'S A GUY SUPPOSED TO GET HIS JACK ON WITH DIAL-UP? TESLA'S WRONG. WHACKING TO VIDEO OR PAPER IS EASIER.
MASTURBATING WHILE LOOKING OVER MY SHOULDER WORRYING MOM WILL COME HOME EARLY. THIS IS HORSESHIT.
I GOTTA FIND A PLACE OF MY OWN. A FEW MORE CHECKS. JUST A FEW. I REFUSE TO BORROW MONEY FROM HER. SHE'S TOO GOOD TO ME ALREADY.
NOW I'M TESTY. TESTY. TESTIS. THERE'S A LINGUISTIC LINK THERE.
COMIX F-K
COMIX L-Q
COMIX A-F
BREEP-BREEP!
HEY. NO, NOTHING. JUST, UH, LOOKING AT SOME APARTMENT LISTINGS.
YEAH, NO, I'M FREE TONIGHT. YEAH, THAT WOULD BE GOOD, ACTUALLY. TOTALLY.
OKAY THEN, YEAH. SEE YOU SOON.
JUST AS WELL I DIDN'T FINISH. MAYBE THERE'S SIGHTLESS LOVEMAKING IN MY--
THE FUCK IS WRONG WITH ME? UNGRATEFUL, SPOILED, BRATTY--
THIS IS A DARK PATCH. I THOUGHT POST-SHE-WHO-WILL-REMAIN-UNNAMED I'D FEEL FREED-UP, MENTALLY.
ALOUD. I'M TALKING TO MYSELF. ALOUD. GREAT. I SHOULD LOOK AT SOME MORE LISTINGS.

7:35 P.M.
T-BONE DINER SINCE 1929 BREAKFAST LUNCH DINNER
T-BONE DINER
GIFTS
T-Bone
OPEN
COCKTAILS
OPEN 24 HRS
SOMETIMES I THINK MY LIFE COULD BE MEASURED BY MEALS IN DINERS. MY EX AND I USED TO-- SORRY. NEVER MIND.
YEAH, I KNOW WHAT YOU MEAN. COULD BE WORSE.
TOO BAD THIS JUKE BOX IS BUSTED. SOME GOOD STUFF: BOB DYLAN, EMMYLOU HARRIS, UNCLE TUPELO, SUZANNE VEGA...
I GATHER YOU'RE NOT A FAN?
DYLAN'S OKAY.
YOU MIND IF I STEAL A FRY OR THREE?
NO, OF COURSE NOT. I'M DONE.
BUT YOU BARELY TOUCHED--
I'M DONE. HELP YOURSELF.
SORRY. SORRY. I DIDN'T MEAN TO SNAP. I'M A LITTLE SENSITIVE ABOUT... FOOD. I USED TO BE VERY...
I WAS FAT. LET'S CALL IT WHAT IT WAS: FAT. I WAS FAT.
SORRY, BUT REAL FAT, OR GIRL-DEFINITION FAT?
FAT-FAT. I WAS LEAD IN A MOVIE. A LITTLE INDIE THING -- UNRELEASED, THANK GOD. I DON'T WANT TO TALK ABOUT IT, BUT MY WEIGHT WAS INTEGRAL TO THE PLOT. I SUPPOSE SOME GOOD CAME OF IT: I TRIMMED DOWN.
SO WHAT I'M SAYING IS: PLEASE, EAT MY FRENCH FRIES.

I **TRY** TO BE SENSITIVE ABOUT-- MY **EX** HAD AN EATING DISORDER. I MEAN--
IT'S OKAY.
YEAH, SO SHE WAS... ANYWAY. *I DON'T WANT TO THINK ABOUT HER.*
IT'S SO STRANGE YOU'RE DIVORCED SO YOUNG.
SO ARE YOU.
UH, YEAH, ABOUT THAT...
motörhead
WE'RE **SEPARATED**, NOT ACTUALLY DIVORCED. BUT IT'S **OVER**. DON'T WORRY ABOUT THAT.
UHHH, OKAY.
NO, **REALLY**. ANYWAY, LET'S GO BACK TO MY PLACE. *THERE'S A CAB!*
TAXI! HEY, TAXI!
THIS IS UNEXPECTED. STILL, CALL ME PRIM, BUT I DON'T WANNA GET **HARD** TWO FEET FROM A DUDE IN A TURBAN. *ONE THAT I AM MAKING EYE CONTACT WITH THROUGH THE REARVIEW MIRROR.*
OKAY, IT JUST GOT **WEIRD**. ***WEIRDER***. I CAN SEE HIS **EYES SMILING**. YUCK. OH BOY, MY HAND IS BETWEEN HER-- JUST *DON'T*-- **TOO LATE**. ***TOTALLY HARD***. YUP. THAT'LL HAPPEN.

RIGHT, LET'S GET UPSTAIRS.
AH, THERE SHE IS, THE ONE WHO'S LATE WITH THE RENT BY SEVERAL DAYS. DO YOU--
HERE! HERE! HAVE IT! LET IT RAIN!
DISGRACEFUL.
OKAY, SO FAR THIS BONER'S ENJOYED THE COMPANY OF A GRINNING SIKH AND AN ANGRY LANDLADY. WHAT NEXT? HOPEFULLY, MAY'S GIRLPARTS.
BUT CASH IS CASH. TILL NEXT MONTH, MISSY!
YEAH, YEAH! MMPH OKAY. SMOOCH GET IN THE LOCK, DARN IT!
JINGLE-JINGLE-- K-CLINK-CLACK
I KNOW YOU WERE BUMMED WE DID IT IN THE DARK, BUT--
NO, NO, NOT AT ALL.
--I'VE GOT A LOT OF ISSUES WITH MY BODY. SO IT'S--
NO NEED. YOUR BODY IS AWESOME.

AND HUZZAH: SHE STANDS BEFORE ME IN THE LIGHT AND LOOKS FANTASTIC. HAVEN'T SEEN THE REAR, BUT... OH JEEZ, FEELS AMAZING.
THAT IS A LOT OF ASS. BUT TRY CONVINCING A WOMAN THAT'S A GOOD THING.
SATURDAY
OH GOD IT'S BEEN AGES SINCE ANYONE--
WHOA. THAT IS A LOT OF BUSH. I SHOULD HAVE KNOWN, WHAT WITH THE FOLK MUSIC. NO BIG. TRIMMED IS NICE BUT SO IS NATURAL.
YEAH, EAT MY FRENCH FRIES. OH YEAH, EAT MY-- GASP
OKAY, THAT'S A LITTLE WEIRD. I'M SO USED TO SYL-- SHE-WHO-WILL-REMAIN-UNNAMED'S PUSSY. HERS WAS SO-- DISCRETE.
MAY'S IS FULL-ON HIPPIE PUSSY. UNRULY PUBES, GENEROUS HELPING OF LABIA. AND HELLO: BIG CLIT. NOT VANESSA DEL RIO BIG, BUT BIG.
I WANT YOU INSIDE ME.
UH...
IDIOT! YOU FORGOT THE CONDOMS! YOU ARE KING SHITBRAIN OF MOUNT NO-FUCK!
IT'S OKAY, I GOT CONDOMS.
AND SO...

WOW. YOU ARE AN AWESOME LAY. YEAH, THAT WAS-- YEAH. HEY, MIND IF I SPARK UP?
HUH?
WEED. WOULD IT BOTHER YOU IF I--
NO, NO. BY ALL MEANS.
EXCELLENT. IT'S BLUEBERRY. REALLY SUPERB HERB. SWEET AND FRUITY. MY GUY HAS THE KINDEST BUD. I ASSUME YOU--
NO, BUT DON'T LET THAT STOP YOU. IT'S NOT GONNA BOTHER YOU SMOKING ALONE, IS IT?
MAYBE A LITTLE. SSSUCK I DON'T THINK ANYONE I'VE EVER BEEN WITH HAS NOT PARTAKEN.
PFFFFF-- COFF-COFF
SORRY. COFF-COFF SOMETIMES WHEN I INHALE-- COFF-COFF
ASSESSING: SEX, AWESOME. ASS, A-PLUS. POT AND SUBSEQUENT COUGHING, RED FLAG.
LOOMING DEADLINE. CAN I AFFORD TO SPEND THE NIGHT? I GOT LIKE ZERO SLEEP LAST TIME.
OH, BRAIN, I HATE YOU SO MUCH.
COFF-COFF CAN YOU STAY THE NIGHT? I HOPE SO. I DON' WANNA--
SNOR-ZZZZ
SCREW THE DEADLINE. POT OR NO POT, YOU GONNA ABANDON THAT? MAY'S A SWEET GIRL. I'M SURE WE'LL FIND SOMETHING IN COMMON SOON.

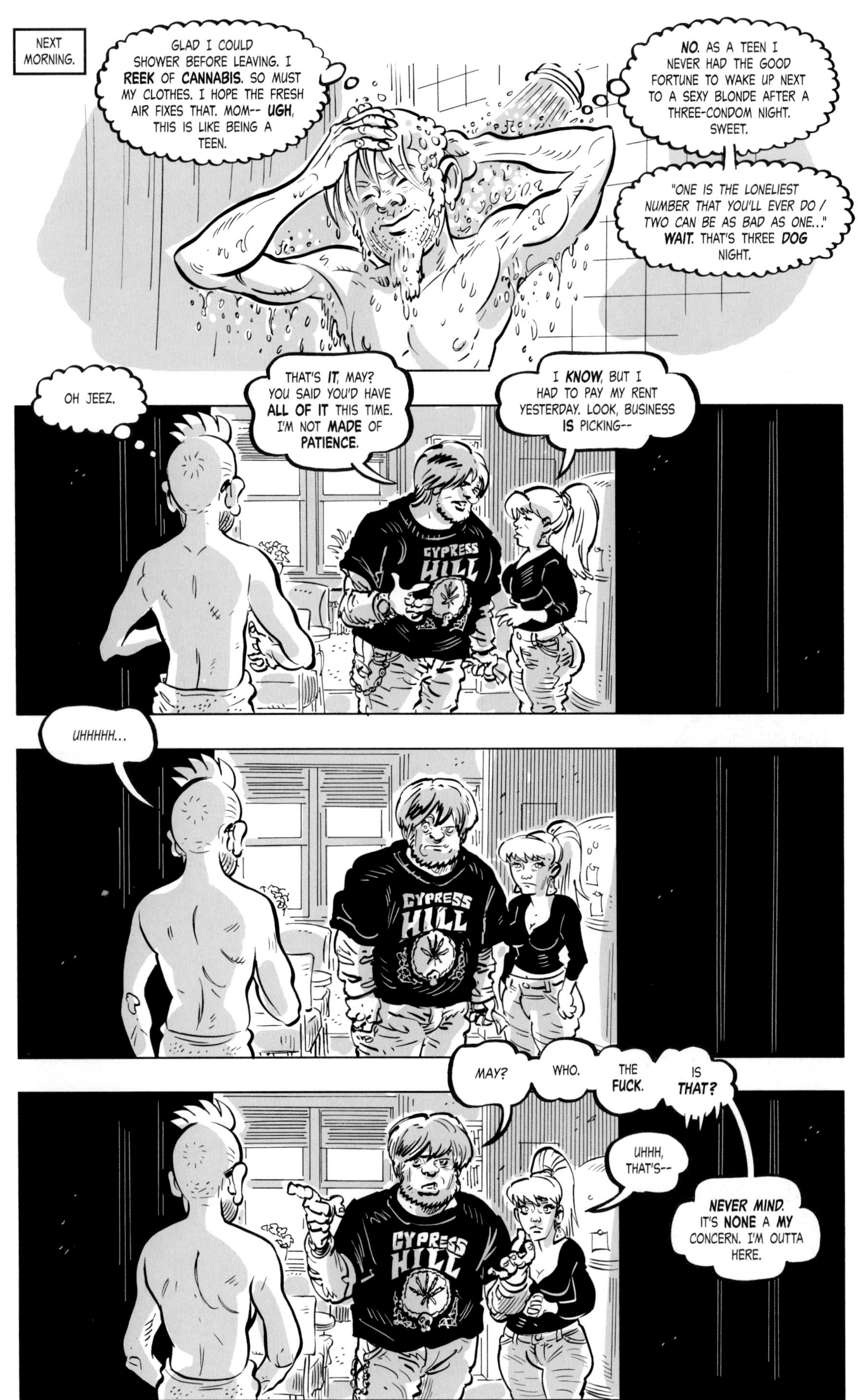
NEXT MORNING.
GLAD I COULD SHOWER BEFORE LEAVING. I REEK OF CANNABIS. SO MUST MY CLOTHES. I HOPE THE FRESH AIR FIXES THAT. MOM-- UGH, THIS IS LIKE BEING A TEEN.
NO. AS A TEEN I NEVER HAD THE GOOD FORTUNE TO WAKE UP NEXT TO A SEXY BLONDE AFTER A THREE-CONDOM NIGHT. SWEET.
"ONE IS THE LONELIEST NUMBER THAT YOU'LL EVER DO / TWO CAN BE AS BAD AS ONE..." WAIT. THAT'S THREE DOG NIGHT.
OH JEEZ.
THAT'S IT, MAY? YOU SAID YOU'D HAVE ALL OF IT THIS TIME. I'M NOT MADE OF PATIENCE.
I KNOW, BUT I HAD TO PAY MY RENT YESTERDAY. LOOK, BUSINESS IS PICKING--
CYPRESS HILL
UHHHHH...
CYPRESS HILL
MAY?
WHO.
THE FUCK.
IS THAT?
UHHH, THAT'S--
NEVER MIND. IT'S NONE A MY CONCERN. I'M OUTTA HERE.
CYPRESS HILL

JUST PAY ME WHAT YOU OWE ME, MAY!
SLAM!
UHHHH... THAT YOUR, UM, POT CONNECTION?
SORT OF. IT'S... COMPLICATED. HE FRONTED THE MONEY FOR MY JEWELRY BUSINESS. I'M STILL PAYING HIM OFF. BUT HE ALSO SUPPLIES MY WEED.
IS HE SOME KIND OF LOAN SHARK OR SOME OTHER UNDERWORLD TYPE? HE'S KIND OF A SCARY DUDE.
I DUNNO. MAYBE. A LITTLE.
HE'S MY HUSBAND. EX. ALMOST.
FLOP!
SO...
COFFEE?

MONDAY, JUNE 19TH. 2:10 A.M.
SO, THE PROS: SHE HAS A BANGING BODY, IS NICE AND KIND AND THE SEX IS GOOD. THE CONS: THE HIPPIE THATCH, THE WEED, THE COUNTRY/FOLK MUSIC AND THE HUSBAND.
LET'S FOCUS ON THE HUSBAND. THE OTHER STUFF'S FINE. I SHOULDN'T'VE MENTIONED THE PUBES. IT'S JUST YOU AN' YOUR PENCHANT FOR SMOOTH.
YOU DID THE RIGHT THING. WE SHARE. IT'S PART OF OUR BOND: NO SECRETS.
YEAH. BUT NOW I REALLY DON'T WANT YOU TO MEET HER.
WHY? YOU AFRAID I'M GONNA BLURT, TOURETTE'S-LIKE, "HI MAY. SO, I HEAR YOU HAVE A MOUND OF SPANISH MOSS ON YOUR MONS."
NO, I S'POSE NOT. SHE IS NICE. BUT OTHER THAN HER WANTING TO SPEND TIME WITH ME I'M NOT SURE WE HAVE ANYTHING IN COMMON.
YOU DON'T EVEN WANNA SPEND TIME WITH YOU.
TRUE. WE GOT NOTHIN' IN COMMON, THEN.
AT LEAST YOU HAVE THE SEX.
AIM IS TRUE
ON ... RECORDS AND TAPES
METALLICA
SIGH
BUT YOU'VE GOT PHILDICKIAN KIPPLEIZATION TO KEEP YOU COMPANY. THE MOUNDS OF SCHTUFF GROW AND GROW EXPONENTIALLY.
I'D SAY, "UP YOURS," BUT YEAH: COLLYER BROS., V2.O. CAN'T EVEN TAKE SOLACE IN WHITE CASTLE. LOCAL ONE'S GONE. THE NEIGHBORHOOD IS CHANGING.
UP

ONE THING HASN'T CHANGED: SHE STILL LIVES AROUND HERE.
I SEE HER ON THE STREET FROM TIME TO TIME. SHE LOOKS RIGHT PAST ME AND I HONOR THE SNUB.
HOW'S SHE LOOK? NO, DON'T ANSWER THAT. I DON'T CARE.
YEAH, YOU DO. YOU FINALLY ACTUALLY DIVORCED?
STILL WAITING ON THE FINAL PAPERS. BUT IT'S DONE. WE'RE OFFICIALLY, LEGALLY, OVER.
UNLIKE MAY AND HER THUGGISH NOT-QUITE-EX. I'D BE CAREFUL, CHUM. WOULDN'T WANT A POST HEADLINE IN YOUR FUTURE.
JESUS, IS THAT THE TIME? I GOTTA GO. IS THE R EVEN RUNNING THIS TIME OF NIGHT?
YOU CAN CATCH A BUS, THEN TRANSFER. OR YOU COULD SPEND THE NIGHT.
I APPRECIATE THAT, BUT THAT'S OKAY. I NEED MY OWN BED. MY OWN PILLOW.
I'LL WAIT FOR THE BUS WITH YOU. I NEED TO PICK UP MILK, ANYWAY.
IT MIGHT BE A WHILE. YOU MIGHT NOT GET HOME UNTIL DAWN.
YOU'RE RIGHT. FUCK IT, I'M TAKING A CAR SERVICE.
GONNA BE PRICEY.
I'LL SPLURGE. MY "LUXURY" OF THE MONTH.
SIGH

AND SO...
JACK IS MUCH MORE COMFORTABLE HUGGING THAN I AM. WHY? AM I EMBARRASSED TO HUG MY BEST FRIEND IN FRONT OF A CAR SERVICE DRIVER? YESSIREE.
--ROAD, REGO PARK. YOU KNOW HOW TO GET THERE?
YEAH, NO SWEAT. I THINK IT'S GREAT, YOU GUYS.
HUH?
YOU GAYS HUGGIN' LIKE IT AIN'T NO THING. S'TERRIFIC. PLUS WHICH, YOU GUYS ALWAYS RAISE PROPERTY VALUES AN' SUCH.
I'M N--
METALLICA
THIS 'HOOD'S BEEN GOIN' DOWNHILL, ARABS AN' SUCH MOVIN' IN AN' THE LIKE. LOTTA LITTER AN' SUCH. BUT YOU HOMOS -- IZZAT OKAY T'SAY? -- KEEP IT TIDY AN' WHATNOT.
I'M N--
AH, FUCK IT. HE WALKS AN INTERESTING LINE BETWEEN TOTAL BIGOT AND OPENMINDED.
WHEN I WAS COMIN' UP AN' SUCH TH' NABE WAS A LOTTA NORWEGIANS. NORWEGIANS! LIKE THE VIKINGS AN' SUCH. S'LIKE ANCIENT HISTORY. YOU EVAH LOOK AT GREEK STATUARY? EVERYONE LOOKS LIKE A FREAKIN' MODEL.
METALLICA
THEN TH' BLOODLINE GOT POLLUTED BY ROMANS. BUT THE GREEKS -- IN THOSE DAYS, WHEN WOMEN WAS SECONDHAND CITIZENS -- IT WAS MORE PRESTIGIOUS TO DO IT WITH A GUY. THEY DIDN' MAKE A THING OF IT.
OH, OH! LOST MY TRAIN. SO GREEKS KINDA TOOK THIS NABE FROM THE NORWEGIANS. MY FOLKS WAS FROM MALTA. BUT THE GAYS. THEY MAKE IT NICE.
UH. SO, YOU AN' BALDIE IN A COMMITTED THING OR YOU MAYBE...?
I'M NOT GAY. IT WAS JUST A HUG.
TALLICA

--JUST A LITTLE BI-CURIOUS! IZZAT SO WRONG?!?
I THOUGHT ONLY MATT--
TUESDAY, JUNE 20TH.
--GOT HIT ON BY CABBIES. HORNING IN ON MY THING, HUH, CHAMPERS?
OH! FUCK YOU! FUCK! YOU! YEAH, BITCH! SUCK IT! FUCK!
YEAH, SO A CABBIE WANTED TO TOSS KOB'S SALAD?
FUCK YOU! UNH-UH, NO. NO! NO YOU DID NOT! FUCK YOU!
I CAN'T SEE THE APPEAL OF THIS THING. MAYBE SOMEDAY WHEN THE GRAPHICS ARE BETTER.
BUDDA-BUDDA-BUDDA! PYOO-PYOO-PYOO!
THESE GRAPHICS ARE CUTTING EDGE, SON. DID ASTEROIDS LOOK THIS GOOD? FROGGER? SPACE INVADERS?
NO, WHICH IS WHY I NEVER PLAYED ANY OF THOSE. THAT AND THE FACT THAT ARCADES SMELL LIKE FEET, TAINT AND SORROW.
WHATEVER. UCCH, SO WHAT? WHAT IS UP FOR KOBS? WHAT IS KOBS'S NEXT MOVE? YOU GETTIN' A PLACE OR LIVING WITH YOUR MOMS FOREV'S?
AND WHO PAYS FOR THIS PLACE?
OH NO YOU DID NOT. I PAY. ME. WITH MY MONEY THAT I HAVE. FROM INVEST-MENTS AND PROPERTIES AND--
I WAS JUST JOSHING.
I DON'T LIKE THAT KINDA JOSHING. I'M NO LEECH. MY A-HOLE BROTHER'S A LEECH. HIM. NOT ME, BRO. NOT ME.
GOTCHA. SORRY. HEY, I GOTTA GO. DEADLINES.
I GET IT. TOSS ME AWAY LIKE A POST-JACK KLEENEX. I SHALL MISS YE FIERCELY.
GODZILLA

OH, YOU WANT SOME? HUH, FUCKER? AND YOU? OH SHIT YEAH, PLENTY OF BULLETS FOR EVERYONE! THE MATT-STERMINATOR IS ON THE CASE!
SO, LATER, I GUESS.
NOTE TO SELF: NEVER GET INVOLVED WITH VIDEO GAMES.
BUDDA-BUDDA-BUDDA! PYOO-PYOO
HEY, MOM. GOTTA GET BACK TO THE BOARD.
HANG ON A SECOND. WE NEED TO TALK.
ARE YOU BREAKING UP WITH ME?
THAT'S A JOKE. BUT YOU'RE NOT LAUGHING. ARE YOU TOSSING ME OUT?
AS IF I WOULD EVER. BUT THE WAY YOU'RE COMING AND GOING? WHILE YOU'RE UNDER THIS ROOF AGAIN THERE NEED TO BE SOME... GUIDELINES. I HESITATE TO SAY RULES, BUT LET'S CALL A SPADE A SPADE.
YOU'RE AN ADULT, BUT I STILL WORRY. YOU SOMETIMES DISAPPEAR FOR A DAY OR SO AT A TIME WITHOUT CHECKING IN. I KNOW IT'S "NOT COOL" TO CALL MOMMY, BUT A LITTLE CONSIDERATION IS ALL I ASK. YOU HAVE A CELL PHONE. USE IT. FAIR?
MORE THAN FAIR. SORRY, MA.
NOW GET BACK TO DRAWING WHATEVER YOU DRAW AND DON'T WANT ME TO SEE.
KIDDING.
I WISH YOU WERE KIDDING.
DRAWING PORN UNDER MOM'S ROOF. I GOTTA GET OUT OF HERE.
HI, MAY. NO, NOTHING. JUST GOT IN. GOTTA GET SOME-- NO, SURE I CAN COME OVER LATER.
KLIK
MOM, I'M GOING OUT LATER! NOT SURE IF I'LL BE BACK TONIGHT, OKAY?
PERFECT. THANK YOU!
BREEP-BREEP!

HUH? WHAT'S THIS?
"Dear Mr. Hoffman, Recently your adult comic, Nicotina, has come to my attention. Though the subject matter is obviously not what we're looking for, your style would lend itself well to our property, Pubescent Radioactive Ikko-ikki Xiphosurans, AKA: PRIX. If you would be interested in joining the fun and frantic world of PRIX, please get back to me. Thanks, Bill Pepito."
WOW. I'M NOT EXACTLY A FAN, BUT THAT'S REGULAR MAINSTREAM COMICS. THAT COULD LIFT ME OUT OF THE SKIN MAG CESSPOOL. RESPONSE TO MR. PEPITO: A BIG "HELL YEAH."
HEY, MA, SOME EDITOR WANTS ME TO WORK FOR HIM DOING PRIX, THE ADVENTURE COMIC FOR KIDS.
THAT'S GREAT. UH, IT'S CALLED "PRICKS", THOUGH?
P-R-I-X. PUBESCENT RADIOACTIVE IKKO-IKKI XIPHOSURANS. THEY'RE MUTANT HORSESHOE CRABS. IT STARTED OFF KINDA UNDERGROUNDY, BUT KIDS LOVE 'EM.
OHHH-KAY. AND YOU'LL BE ABLE TO SHOW ME. NIFTY.
NOT THAT I'VE EVER DREAMED OF DOING A FRANCHISE BOOK, BUT IT'LL BE NICE TO BE ABLE TO SHOW MOM WHAT I DO FOR A CHANGE.
WELL, BACK TO INKING TITTIES. FOR NOW.
INKING TITTIES. THINKING TITTIES. WILL I EVER SEE MAY'S? SEEN EVERYTHING ELSE. THIS IS SOME KIND OF INTERNAL MOBIUS STRIP OF NIPPULAR BOOBULAR DIMENSIONS. MY WORK DOESN'T GET ME GOING, BUT THINKING ABOUT MAY...
FIGHT IT. FIGHT IT. THINK ABOUT MARTIAL ARTS-EXPERT HORSESHOE CRABS.
TITS. DAMMIT.

THAT'S GREAT NEWS. EVERYONE'S HEARD OF PRIX. MY NEPHEW LOVES 'EM.
IT'S KIND OF BRILLIANT MARKETING: "SILLY PARENTS, PRIX ARE FOR KIDS!" IS A GREAT SLOGAN.
T-BONE DINER
IFTS
T-Bone
OPEN
COCKTAILS
OPEN
I FEEL A LITTLE SELF-CONSCIOUS BEING THE ONLY ONE EATING.
I ATE WITH MY MOM. SORRY. SHE COOKED SO I DIDN'T WANT TO--
DOES THAT SEEM MAMA'S BOY-ISH?
NO, IT SEEMS GOOD SON-ISH. I LIKE THAT YOU LIKE YOUR MOM. MEN WHO LIKE THEIR MOMS TEND TO BE NICER TO WOMEN.
MY EX DOESN'T LIKE HIS MOTHER. NOT THAT SHE'S LIKABLE, BUT STILL.
BUT LET'S FOCUS ON YOUR GOOD NEWS. DID YOU LIKE PRIX AS A KID?
TO HEAR YOU SAY IT, IT IS A WEIRD ACRONYM FOR A KIDS' THING. BUT NO, I WAS ALREADY A TEEN WHEN IT DEBUTED.
YOU'RE WHAT, AGAIN: TWENTY-FIVE?
YEAH. AND YOU'RE TWENTY-SEVEN, RIGHT? SO, SAME THING: TOO OLD FOR PRIX.
AND SO...
NEVER TOO OLD FOR PRIX.
I BELIEVE THAT IS A SINGLE-ENTENDRE.

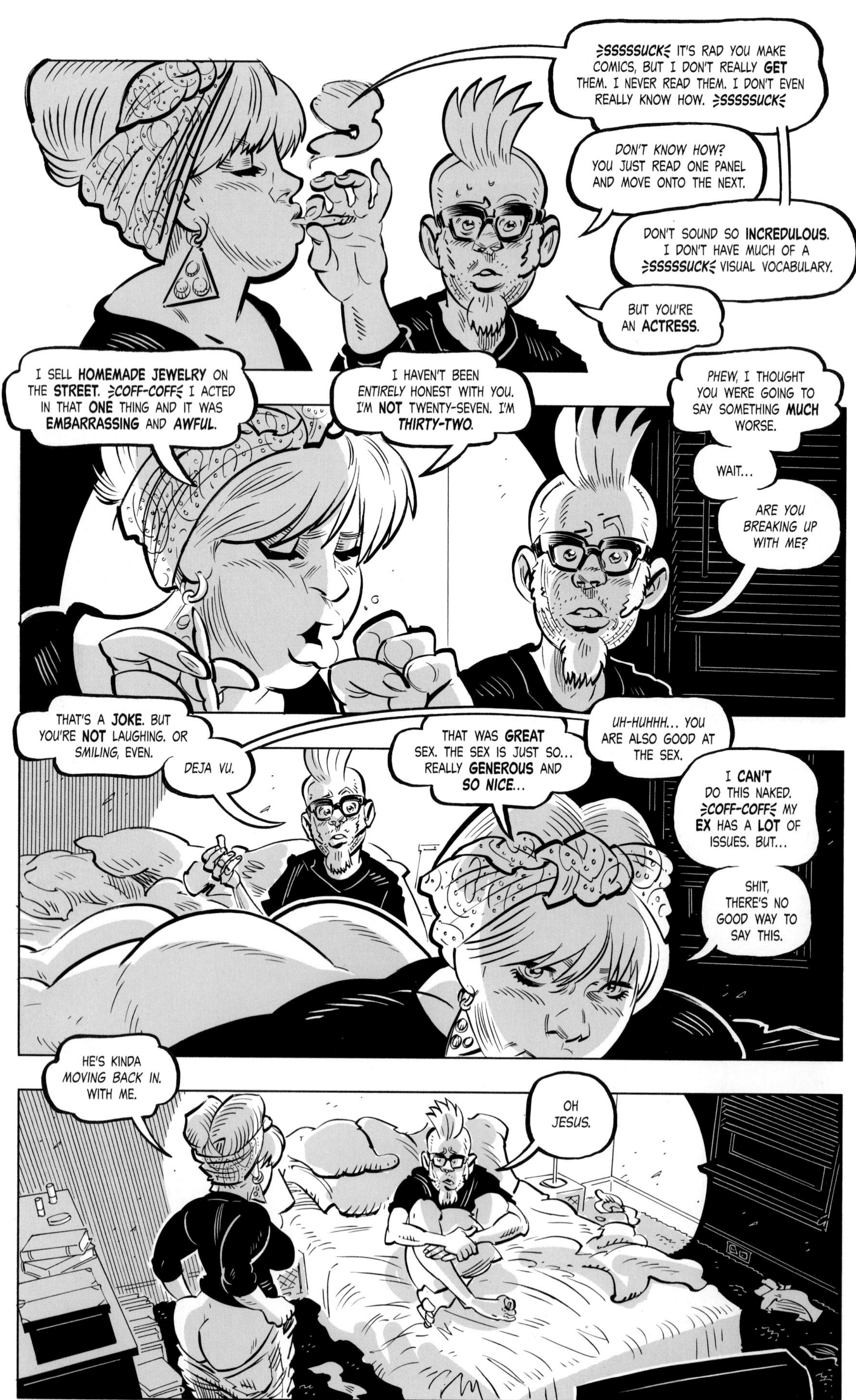

⋟SSSSSUCK⋞ IT'S RAD YOU MAKE COMICS, BUT I DON'T REALLY GET THEM. I NEVER READ THEM. I DON'T EVEN REALLY KNOW HOW. ⋟SSSSSUCK⋞
DON'T KNOW HOW? YOU JUST READ ONE PANEL AND MOVE ONTO THE NEXT.
DON'T SOUND SO INCREDULOUS. I DON'T HAVE MUCH OF A ⋟SSSSSUCK⋞ VISUAL VOCABULARY.
BUT YOU'RE AN ACTRESS.
I SELL HOMEMADE JEWELRY ON THE STREET. ⋟COFF-COFF⋞ I ACTED IN THAT ONE THING AND IT WAS EMBARRASSING AND AWFUL.
I HAVEN'T BEEN ENTIRELY HONEST WITH YOU. I'M NOT TWENTY-SEVEN. I'M THIRTY-TWO.
PHEW, I THOUGHT YOU WERE GOING TO SAY SOMETHING MUCH WORSE.
WAIT...
ARE YOU BREAKING UP WITH ME?
THAT'S A JOKE. BUT YOU'RE NOT LAUGHING. OR SMILING, EVEN.
DEJA VU.
THAT WAS GREAT SEX. THE SEX IS JUST SO... REALLY GENEROUS AND SO NICE...
UH-HUHHH... YOU ARE ALSO GOOD AT THE SEX.
I CAN'T DO THIS NAKED. ⋟COFF-COFF⋞ MY EX HAS A LOT OF ISSUES. BUT...
SHIT, THERE'S NO GOOD WAY TO SAY THIS.
HE'S KINDA MOVING BACK IN. WITH ME.
OH JESUS.

I'M STILL WEARING A CONDOM.

1:15 A.M.
I APPRECIATE YOU LETTING ME COME OVER.
WHAT WAS I GOING TO DO, SAY NO?
WELL, REJECTION SEEMS TO BE TONIGHT'S THEME.
DON'T THINK LIKE THAT. HEY, THERE ARE PLENTY OF OTHER--
I DON'T NEED A PEP TALK, I JUST DIDN'T WANNA GO HOME TO MY MOM'S AFTER THAT. I CAN ONLY FEEL LIKE SO MUCH OF A LOSER IN ONE NIGHT.
YOU'RE NOT A LOSER. SHE MADE A BAD CHOICE. SHE PICKED WRONG. BESIDES, DIDN'T YOU SAY YOU HAD LIKE NOTHING IN COMMON?
YEAH. BUT SHE WAS NICE.
THAT WORD AGAIN. LIKE I SAID: PUPPIES ARE NICE. BLAND THINGS ARE NICE. AND DON'T SAY I'M NOT.
THAT WAS A JOKE. YOU'RE A GOOD DUDE. YOU'RE A GOOD PERSON.
WE BOTH ARE.
SO WHY'RE WE PAINFULLY SINGLE? WOEFULLY, PAINFULLY, MISERABLY SINGLE?
PSYCHOPATH
REMIND ME TO NOT PICK UP NEXT TIME YOU CALL LATE AT NIGHT.
ROLLING ROCK

SATURDAY, JUNE 24TH, NOONISH.
BUBELEH! THIS'LL BE A GOOD PERK-ME-UP FOR YOU. FRANK'S PSYCHED TO SEE YOU AND WE CAN ALWAYS USE SOME SPARE HANDS-- LITERALLY!
I JUST NEED SOME DISTRACTION FROM FEELING REJECTED.
WELL, NO ONE'S GONNA REJECT YOU HERE!
BEAR HUG FOR THE BOY! NOW LET'S GET INSIDE, WHERE IT'S COOL. I'M CHAFING LIKE A BEAR UNDER THIS FARKAKTE SMOCK.
I DON'T THINK I CAN DO THIS.
MAHVAD QUVHA' SOH!
I DON'T MEAN TO DISHONOR ANYONE.
IT'S DIFFERENT WHEN IT'S JUST US OR AT A CON, BUT THIS-- THERE ARE CAMERAS. I CAN'T DO IT.
DAVID, COME ON-- I MEAN, MAGHWI'!
HE HAS FORSAKEN US.
AND THERE GOES OUR RIDE. QEYLIS VA.
(WE ARE SO LUCKY TO HAVE WITNESSED THAT.)

ROB! HEY-HEY, BRI' SAID YOU'D BE LENDING A HAND. GOOD GUESTS TODAY: JOEY ZHEE, A CHINESE STANDUP WITH A HARE LIP; THREE FAT KLINGONS--
TWO. ONE OF THEM RABBITED. WELL, WEDGED HIS CHUNKY KEISTER BACK INTO HIS CIVIC AND TOOK OFF. MAGICAL.
CRAP. WELL, TWO KLINGONS IS BETTER THAN NONE.
IS THAT DEPUTY DEEDEE, FROM THE RANGER RIVERS SHOW?
THE SAME. SHE'S OUR "STAR" GUEST.
JEEZ, I HAD THE BIGGEST CRUSH ON HER WHEN I WAS A KID.
YOU NEVER CAME TO ANY OF THE OTHER TAPINGS SHE WAS AT? SHE'S KINDA NUTTY, WHICH IS WHY SHE'S A GREAT GUEST. I'LL INTRODUCE YOU... IN CHARACTER. NONE OF THESE PEOPLE EVER DEAL WITH THE REAL ME, SO REMINDER: NEVER CALL ME FRANK AROUND THE "TALENT." CALL ME HENRY, OR MR. DIMSDALE.
UH, UH, UM, DEPUTY DEEDEE, THIS IS, UH, ROB HOFFMAN. HE'S ONE OF THE, UM, PUPPETEERS. HE'S ALSO AN, UM, ARTIST.
AN ARTIST AND A PUPPETEER. MY MY. I WAGER YOU HAVE TALENTED HANDS.
HEH. SOMETIMES. IT'S AN HONOR TO MEET YOU. BIG FAN.
REALLY, NOW? ISN'T THAT SWEET? EXCUSE ME. MUST POWDER MY NOSE BEFORE TAPING COMMENCES.
SHE'S SWEET BUT DOTTY. DEPUTY DOTTY MIGHT BE MORE APROPOS THESE DAYS.
IT ALWAYS UNNERVES ME A BIT WHEN YOU SHIFT FROM NORMAL YOU TO YOUR SHOW PERSONA.
IT PUTS THE GUESTS AT EASE IF I SEEM ILL AT EASE. MY STAMMERING RELAXES THEM.
GODFLESH

HEY, KIMMY. HOW'S IT GOING?
CRAZED. GRAB SOME PUPPETS AND LET'S GET DOWN BEHIND THE COUCH.
THAT SOUNDED **WAY** MORE SUGGESTIVE THAN YOU INTENDED.
YOU'VE BEEN DRAWING DIRTY COMICS FOR TOO LONG, ROB.
FIVE MINUTES, PEOPLE!
ONCE THE MUSIC FADES DOWN, HANK WILL INTRODUCE THE GUESTS. **DEPUTY DEEDEE** IS FIRST, THEN **KLINGON TRIO** -- UH, I MEAN **DUO** -- AND FINALLY **MR. ZHEE**.
BRIAN, AS **PETEY THE PRANCING BABOON**, YOU COME IN AT SOME POINT TO DANCE.
FRANK AND KIMMY SEEM TO HAVE THE **PERFECT** MARRIAGE. THEY'RE BOTH SO INTO KITSCH AND PUPPETS AND WEIRDNESS.
MY GOD THIS **CARPET** IS **DISGUSTING**. WHAT AM I LAYING ON? ***PLEASE*** DON'T LET ME GET **FLEAS**, **SCABIES**, **BED BUGS**--
NOW I'M ITCHY. RELAX. ***RELAX***. JUST **BREATHE**. BUT NOT ***TOO*** DEEP. THIS CARPET SMELLS OF **ASS**.
DO THEY SHOOT THE **NAKED** PUBLIC ACCESS SHOWS IN HERE? *DON'T THINK ABOUT IT.* JUST **DON'T THINK** AT ALL. *SHUT THE FUCK UP ALREADY, BRAIN.*
THREE, TWO, ONE--
AND WE'RE BACK. WELCOME TO ***KINESCOPE KABARET***. AND HOW ARE YOU TODAY, OTTO?
...
I **SEE**. NOT FEELING TOO TALKATIVE, AS USUAL.
...
WELL, WE, UM, HAVE SOME, UM, **GREAT** GUESTS, SO LET'S BRING OUT **DEPUTY DEEDEE BELLE FLEUR**.

--REMINDS ME SO MUCH OF THE REALM OF PRETEND. THESE DELIGHTFUL PUPPETS.
DELIGHTFUL? I GUESS THESE ARE ALMOST AS CREEPY AS THE ONES ON RANGER RIVERS. DEPUTY DEEDEE IS TOTALLY KITCHY-COOING MY PALM.
GAWD, NOT FIVE FEET FROM FRANK'S MISSUS. IS THIS AUTONOMIC OR LIMBIC? BRAIN! C'MON, BRAIN: DON'T SEND BONER SIGNALS DOWNTOWN.
DEEDEE IS REALLY GOING TO TOWN WITH THE LOVEY-DOVEYING ON MR. CAT. AND I'M MAKING HIM RESPOND. I SHOULD JUST WAGGLE THE PUPPET, BUT NO, I'M MAKING HIM RUB HER HAND WITH HIS PAWS. WHO AM I, FUCKING JIM HENSON?
12 MINUTES LATER (40 IN BONER TIME).
...SHASHAYSH INTO SHALON AN' SHAYSH, "THASH NO LADY, THASH MY SHTEAMSHOVEL." SHANK YOU. EVAH NOTISH HOW SHOME PEEPO A'WAYSH SHAY WHASH ON A MINDSH BUT--
OH THANK CHRIST FOR THIS GUY. IF THE KLINGONS WEREN'T, HE'S PURE ANAPHRODISIAC.
SUPER PASSWORD
WIN
SHAY, I NO FINISHSHED YETSH--
DAMNED DIRTY APE, I'LL KILL YOU!
OH NO! PETEY, NOT NOW!
HEY THERE! GEORGIE GIRL / SWINGING DOWN THE STREET SO FANCY FREE...

NO MISSED CALLS. MENTAL SIGH.
I WAS RIGHT, YOU **DO** HAVE **TALENTED HANDS**. NEED A LIFT, YOUNG MAN?
HUH? OH, DID YOU DRIVE?
DID I DRIVE. A **TAXI**, PRECIOUS THING. A **HIRED COACH**.
CITYWIDE STU
GODFLESH
WE'RE HEADING HOME.
YOU COMING, BUBBE?
HORST
DARLING DANCING PRIMATE, ***I*** AM GIVING THIS LAD A RIDE. ***TA-TA!***
I--
HUSH, NOT A WORD OF PROTEST.
COACHMAN, PLEASE TAKE US TO THE **FATTED CAFE** ON FIRST AND 79TH. AND MAKE HASTE, WE'RE **RAVENOUS**.
I DO HOPE YOU'VE AN APPETITE.
UM, YES?
SPLENDID. WITH NOURISHMENT COMES VIGOR. AND STOP FRETTING SO MUCH, DEAR BOY. IT CREASES THE BROW.
GODFLESH

AH, MADAME BELLE FLEUR, SO NICE TO SEE YOU AGAIN. AND WHO IS YOUR NEW COMPANION?
THIS IS YOUNG ROBERT, YES? AN ARTIST AND DEVILISHLY DEXTROUS PUPPETEER.
UH...
WORDS ARE NOT HIS MEDIUM. MY USUAL TABLE, YES?
FOLLOW ME, PLEASE.
The Fatted Café
THE FOOD'S MERELY ADEQUATE, BUT COMING HERE MAKES ME FEEL DEWY PAR COMPARAISON. EVEN IN THE COMPANY OF SUCH A YOUNG ROUGH DIAMOND.
I HAVE TO SAY THIS IS ALL VERY... UNEXPECTED.
"LIFE SHOULD BE AN ADVENTURE."
HEY, THAT'S WHAT YOU SAID ON RANGER RIVERS.
YES. YES I DID.
PERHAPS AFTER THE DELECTABLES YOU MIGHT CARE TO VISIT MY COLLECTION OF ARTIFACTS FROM THE RANGER RIVERS SHOW. I HAVE THE ACTUAL PUPPETS SQUIRRELKIN AND TIGGLEPUSS.
UM, SURE, THAT'D BE INTERESTING.
THIS IS TOO FUCKING WEIRD. IS SHE TRYING TO SEDUCE ME WITH PUPPETS? INTRIGUINGLY MANIPULATIVE.

I HAVE TO SAY, THESE PUPPETS ARE VERY COOL, MS. BELLE FLEUR.
PLEASE, DARLING, PLEASE. YOU MAKE ME FEEL OLD. DEEDEE WOULD BE FINE. EXCUSE ME A MOMENT. MAKE YOURSELF COMFORTABLE.
THESE PUPPETS ARE EVEN CREEPIER IN PERSON. AND I USED TO LOVE "THE REALM OF PRETEND."
JEEZ, IS THAT BLOOD?
DO YOU PARTAKE OF HASHISH? I FIND IT HEIGHTENS THE SENSES AND RELAXES THE MIND. THE SET OF RANGER RIVERS WAS REDOLENT OF IT.
OH GOLLY.
YOU DELIGHT ME. I LOVE TO HEAR A CITIFIED LAD SPEAK BUMPKINESE.
HEY, UM, THIS HAS BEEN--
--PROLOGUE, RO-BAIR. I SAW HOW YOU EYED ME AT THE STUDIO. YOU THINK I DON'T RECOGNIZE "THE LOOK"? I WAS A SWEET GIRL ON A LONG-RUNNING CHILDREN'S SHOW, BUT DON'T MISTAKE THAT FOR REALITY. AN ACTRESS ACTS. A FIRE IS STOKED. AN APPETITE MUST BE FED.
I AM LITERALLY SCARED STIFF. DAMMIT, BRAIN/BONER/LIMBIC/AUTO-NOMIC/WHICHEVER.
AND SO...

YES, OH YES. THE HASHISH TRULY HEIGHTENS EVERY STROKE. YES. PACE YOURSELF. PACE. WE CAN MAKE THIS LAST THROUGH THE DAY AND INTO THE NIGHT.
THIS IS HAPPENING. I'M HAVING SEX WITH SOMEONE I HAD A CRUSH ON WHEN I WAS SIX.
THE WORD "SURREAL" IS OVERUSED, BUT BONING THE FIFTY-ISH INCARNATION OF DEPUTY DEEDEE KINDA COUNTS.
GOOFLESH
RANGER RIVERS WOULD BE PROUD ONE OF HIS TELE-SCOUTS GREW UP TO KNOW HOW TO TREAT A LADY AND HER ATTENDANT ANATOMY.
WOULD HE?!?
GOOFLESH
ARE YOU EARNEST OR LACKING IRONY? RIVERS WAS A LOVELY MAN, BUT SEXLESS AS A RIVERBED BURNISHED SMOOTH BY THE EONS.
I'M NOT EARNEST. IT'S JUST... I JUST FIGURED I'D WIGGLE SOME PUPPETS AROUND AND TAKE MY MIND OFF THINGS.
"THINGS." PLEASE, FEEL FREE TO UNBURDEN YOURSELF. SISTER MARY DEEDEE IS HERE.
I JUST GOT SORT OF DUMPED BY MY SORT OF ALMOST NEW GIRLFRIEND. THAT ON THE HEELS OF SPLITTING WITH MY WIFE.
YOU ARE AN INTERESTING SPECIMEN. THE WAY YOU CARRIED YOURSELF I KNEW THERE WERE SOME MILES ON YOUR YOUTHFUL FRAME. A DIVORCEE SO YOUNG.
YEAH. AND THIS NEW GIRL SAID SHE WAS GETTING A DIVORCE BUT JUST SHACKED BACK UP WITH HER EX.
I OFTEN WISH I COULD MUSTER THE FORTITUDE TO DIVORCE MY LIMP NOODLE OF A HUSBAND.
GOOFLESH
WAIT: WHAT?!? NO, NO, NO.

I AM NOT IN THE CUCKOLDING BUSINESS. HUSBAND? AND WHAT'S HIS DEAL? I'M LIVING SOME RIDICULOUS BEDROOM FARCE.
MY HUSBAND IS A LOVELY MAN, ACTUALLY. VERY REFINED AND LETTERED. BUT HE'S MR. HOLISTIC AND AT THIS STAGE ONLY A JOLT OF MODERN CHEMISTRY WOULD REANIMATE HIS NETHERS.
NO. NYET. I CAN'T KNOW THIS. I DON'T WANNA KNOW THIS. I GOTTA GO!
I TRULY HATE TO SEE YOU LEAVE IN SUCH A STATE. WAS IT REALLY SO TERRIBLE?
NO, IT WAS AWESOME, BUT--
THEN DON'T LEAVE THIS WAY.
I'M OLD ENOUGH TO BE YOUR MOTHER, BUT YOUR ATTENTION MADE ME FEEL DESIRABLE...
GODFLESH
I HAVEN'T FELT THAT IN A WHILE.
I'M SORRY.
DON'T BE SORRY. I'M AN ACTRESS. I PLAYACT. I HAVE FUN WITH THIS PERSONA I'VE CREATED. MY HUSBAND IS IN EGYPT ON A DIG. POKING AT RELICS. HE ENJOYS THAT.
I'M THE ONE RELIC HE DOESN'T ENJOY POKING.
GODFLESH
THERE, THERE. IT'S OKAY.
SNIFF YOU HAVE STRONG ARMS. GOOD FOR PUPPETRY. AND MAKING ART. WHAT KIND OF ART DO YOU DO, ANYWAY?
CARTOONING. I DRAW COMICS.
OH. SO NOT REAL ART, THEN.
OUCH. I SUPPOSE NOT.

PLEASE, BEFORE YOU GO, I WANT YOU TO HAVE SOMETHING.
UM, REALLY, THAT'S NOT NECESSARY.
HERE, PLEASE: A PARTING GIFT. THE GENUINE **TIGGLEPUSS**.
I COULDN'T POSSIBLY--
--**REFUSE**. YOU COULDN'T POSSIBLY **REFUSE**. I **DO** HOPE TO SEE YOU AGAIN. WHAT DO THEY CALL IT? *"FRIENDS WITH BENEFITS?"*
UH, YEAH.
YOU'RE NOT A **REAL** ARTIST. **I'M** NOT A **REAL** ACTRESS. WE MAKE DO, LOVE. *WE MAKE DO.*
ESH
WHAT JUST HAPPENED?
LESH
DAMNED IF I KNOW, KID. BUT PLEASE, *PLEASE*, **PLEASE** JUST GET ME THE FUCK OUT OF HERE.
GODFLESH

MONDAY, JULY 3RD. 12:55 P.M.
...CAN SEE IT'S A GREAT SPACE. VERY ROOMY. AND THERE'S HOW MANY OF YOU, AGAIN?
JUST ME. ONLY ME.
WELL, THEN IT'S A REALLY SPACIOUS SPACE FOR A SINGLE OCCUPANT. VERY ROOMY.
YEAH. YEAH, THERE'S NO SHORTAGE OF SPACE.
KORN
EXACTLY. AND YOU DO WHAT, AGAIN?
GRAPHIC DESIGN.
GREEEEAT. THAT'S REALLY GREAT. ANYTHING I'D KNOW?
I DOUBT IT. JUST, YOU KNOW, COMMERCIAL STUFF. NOTHING EXCITING.
YOU KNOW WHAT? I CAN'T DO THIS AGAIN.
THIS CHARADE. I LIKE THIS APARTMENT. I'M RECENTLY DIVORCED, I'M NOT A GRAPHIC DESIGNER, I DRAW COMICS. I WORK HARD, BUT I'M FREELANCE.
I SEE. DIVORCED, HUH? YOU LOOK--
I'M TWENTY-FIVE. LET'S SAY I MADE MY MISTAKES EARLY. HOPEFULLY GOT THEM OUT OF THE WAY YOUNG.
FREELANCE. HMM. THAT'S ALWAYS A BIT TRICKY. BUT I LIKE YOU.
KORN

I LIKE YOUR HONESTY. I DON'T GET A LOT OF THAT. OR GIVE IT.
I'VE BEEN GETTING MY FINANCES UP TO SNUFF AND I NOW HAVE A NEW GIG THAT SHOULD BE VERY STEADY. YOU EVER HEAR OF PRIX:
PUBESCENT RADIOACTIVE--
--IKKO-IKKI XIPHOSURANS. MY SON LOVES THEM. YOU DRAW THAT?
JUST STARTED. BUT IT'S A REGULAR GIG.
KoЯn
CAN MY SON GET A SNEAK PEEK OF THE COMICS BEFORE THEY COME OUT?
SURE, I COULD MAKE THAT HAPPEN.
THE MANAGEMENT HATES FREELANCERS, BUT THIS 'HOOD COULD USE SOME ARTISTIC PEOPLE. I'LL WORK MY MAGIC.
YOU DO THAT AND I'LL TOTALLY HOOK YOUR SON UP.
KoЯn
I'LL BE IN TOUCH TO LET YOU KNOW IF MY MAGIC WORKED. HAVE A HAPPY FOURTH!
YOU, TOO. THANKS, TAMMY.
PLEASE LET THIS HAPPEN. I CAN MANAGE THIS PLACE. WHAT I CAN'T MANAGE IS TRAIPSING TO A DOZEN OR SO MORE.
WAS SHE FLIRTING WITH ME? COULD I DATE A WOMAN WITH A KID? ANSWERS: NO AND NO. GO HOME AND GET TO WORK DRAWING PRIX AND PRICKS.
KoЯn
I ALWAYS SEEM TO BE BALANCING PORN AND KID STUFF. BUT PRIX AND PRICKS BEAT DAFT ANY DAY.
FRAMING
PHOTOSONIC
1Hour Studio
LORRE
REGO PARK
SHOPORIUM
BIG DEAL!
$15.99
RadioSha
RadioShack

7:45 P.M.

YOU NEVER NOTICED THEY LOOK LIKE **DICKS**? **YOU**, ROBELEH? **YOU?** OF **ALL** PEOPLE?

TOWER DINER

A PROPERTY CREATED BY **STONER OUTSIDERS** THAT'S THE **BIGGEST** KIDS' THING SINCE **MICKEY MOUSE**. YET THEY'RE **GLANS** AT A **GLANCE**.

SO, YOU'RE STAYING IN THE REGO. YAY.

NO GUARANTEE. SHE SAID SHE'D **TRY** TO GET ME IN THERE. BUT YEAH, MERE BLOCKS AWAY.

SO YEAH, YEAH, APARTMENT, BLAH-BLAH PRIX. LAST WE SAW YOU YOU WERE ACCEPTING A RIDE FROM DEPUTY DEEDEE.
I'VE SEEN YOU SINCE THEN, HAVEN'T I?
YOU HAVEN'T. IT'S ALMOST AS IF YOU'VE BEEN DUCKING US, BUBELEH. SPILL. YOU DID, DIDN'T YOU?
BASED ON THE DEFENDANT'S SILENCE AND BODY LANGUAGE...
DOES THE DEFENDANT WISH TO PLEAD OTHERWISE?
AUUGH
GUILTY AS CHARGED.
YOU GOT IN A TAXI WITH HER, TRAVELED ACROSS TOWN IN A HEIGHTENED STATE OF ANTICIPATION. YOU--
FINE. ENOUGH ALREADY. IT HAPPENED, OKAY? I FUCKED DEPUTY DEEDEE! YOU HAPPY NOW?
YOU WHAT?!? WE JUST ASSUMED YOU'D SHARED AN AWKWARD BRUNCH. SHE'S SUCH A SERIAL FLIRT WE JUST TOOK IT FOR AFFECT.
OH JESUS. I--
OF COURSE YOU SCHTUPPED HER. NOW EAT YOUR FOOD, BUBBE, IT'S GETTING COLD.
I HATE YOU SO MUCH.
YOU LOVE ME.

THURSDAY, JULY 6TH, 9:42 A.M.
BREEP-BREEP!
FUGGIN' PHONE... TIME IZZIT--
AHEM-AHEM
HELLO? WHAT? NO, I'S AWAKE. RIGHT, RIGHT: HONESTY.
NO, I WAS ASLEEP, TAMMY. I KEEP LATE HOURS. UH-HUH.
COSIGNER ON THE LEASE? NO, I UNDERSTAND. NO, NOT A PROBLEM. COOL. THANK YOU. YEAH, NO, I'M EXCITED.
YES, I AM GOING TO GO BACK TO SLEEP. HA, RIGHT. SEE YOU AT THE OFFICE TO SIGN. TWO CHECKS. YUP. BYE.
LIKE I'M GONNA BE ABLE TO FALL BACK ASLEEP. I GOT THE APARTMENT. THAT'S AWESOME. I'LL JUST LIE HERE FOR A FEW TO LET IT SINK IN.
ZZZZZZZZZZZZZZZZ

2:30 P.M.
THE POLE IN THE HOLE, THE POLE IN THE HOLE. BUT SOON YOU'LL BE ROLLIN' IN MUTANT HORSESHOE CRAB LUCRE.
NOT QUITE. PAGE RATE'S ABOUT HALF WHAT I GET FROM YOU GUYS.
WORD IS, CUTS ARE COMING, SO SOON IT'LL BE ADIOS, SMUTTY COMICS.
SO FOR ONCE I'M AHEAD OF THE EIGHT BALL.
SURE, WHY NOT? HEY, GOT YOU A HOUSEWARMING GIFT FOR YOUR NEW CRIB.
A KIND BUD ASHTRAY? GEE, THANKS.
YOU'RE WELCOME. DIDN'T YOU SAY YOUR NEW GAL-PAL PARTAKES OF THE JOLLY GREEN?
SHE GOT BACK WITH HER EX.
OOPS. SORRY, GUY. MY HEART WAS IN THE RIGHT PLACE. NO SELF-RESPECTING MAN SHOULD BE WITHOUT AN ASHTRAY. NOT EVEN A NONSMOKER.
OH, NEWSFLASH: I'M TAKING THE GIG AS M.E. AT KIND BUD.
SO, ROB, WHILE WE'RE STILL SPENDING, WANNA FINALLY DRAW BIG DONG FOR ME FO' CASH DOLLAH BILLS?
FUNNY HOW THINGS SAID HERE WOULD QUALIFY AS HARASSMENT ANYWHERE ELSE.
GOOD THING THE RULES ARE EVEN LAXER AT K.B..

WANNA GRAB SOME LUNCH?
YEAH, I COULD EAT.
AND NOW THE HARASSMENT REALLY BEGINS.
BLOW ME.
SEE? SEE?
YOU KNOW I'M JUST FUCKING WITH YOU, RIGHT? I'M A MARRIED WOMAN.
I'M NOT GETTING INVOLVED WITH ANY MORE OF THOSE. THANKS FOR TELLING ME, THOUGH.
OH YEAH? SPILL.
SINCE THE END OF MY OWN, I'VE INADVERTENTLY BEEN WITH TWO MARRIED WOMEN.
OOF. WOMEN, HUH?
SO, THE THING I'M NOT KIDDING ABOUT IS DRAWING DONG FOR MY GAY -- I MEAN TOTALLY STRAIGHT NUDIE MAG FOR WOMEN.
SIGH UH, SAME RATES SAMMY PAYS?
HIGHER. AHH, YEAH, BOYEE, NOW YOU'RE LISTENING. THIS IS ILLUSTRATION RATES, NOT COMICS. LESS WORK, MORE PAY.
I'LL HATE MYSELF LATER, BUT SOUNDS LIKE EASY MONEY. BUT I'M USING AN ALIAS.
COOL BEANS. AND NOW I'LL KNOW WHAT YOUR THANG LOOKS LIKE 'CAUSE ARTISTS TEND TO USE THEIR OWN AS A MODEL.
AND YOU'D KNOW THIS HOW? JUST FOR THAT, THEY'LL ALL HAVE THOSE DROOPY DRAWSTRING FORSKS.
UGH. HEY, SOME FOLKS DIG THAT.

FRIDAY, JULY 7TH, 9:45 P.M.
HA! MY BOY KOBS DRAWING MAYONNAISE PENS FOR MUH-NAY. ART HOOKER HOFFBRAU!
FUCK YOU, FUCKER! HAIL O' LEAD! HA!
I DON'T THINK I CAN SIT IDLY BY AS YOU MASSACRE LEGIONS OF VIRTUAL ENEMIES. I'M GONNA SPLIT.
BUDDA-BUDDA-BUDDA! PYOO-PYOO-PYOO!
NO-NO! GAME OVER! FUCK IT, LET'S GO DO SOMETHING. KOBBA NEEDS TO FIND LOVE. LET'S DITCH AND HIT SOME NIGHTSPOTS.
I'M NOT EXACTLY DRESSED--
TUT-TUT! PISH-POSH, EH WOT? YOU LOOKIN' FINE AS FROG HAIR, CHAPPY. LET'S CALL MAX AN' HIT THE CLUBS!
I DUNNO IF I--
--SHOULD BE HERE. I'M NOT EXACTLY ATTIRED IN "CREATURE OF THE NIGHT" MODE.
I'M SURE SOME VAMPIRESS HERE WILL FIND YOUR ACCOUTREMENT FETCHINGLY INCONGRUOUS.
I DOUBT THAT VERY MUCH.
DO NOT BE MAXIE-BUZZKILL. WE ARE MAKING SURE KOBS GETS HIS HOOSH MOIST TONIGHT! FACT.

ROUND ONE.
TO KOBS AND REVERSING HIS SHIT LUCK WITH SOME FRESH POO-SAY TONIGHT!
BECAUSE GIRLS ARE LOOKING FOR BITTER YOUNG DIVORCEES. WHATEVER.
N-N-N-N-NO. NOT "WHATEVER," DUDE. YES! YES! NO MORE MRS. ROBINSONS, BITCH. HOT YOUNG FLESH FOR FRANKENSTEIN. TOAST TO THAT SHIT! L'CHAIM!
TINK
WHATEV--
SKOAL.
AND THERE HE GOES. YOU THINK HE'LL DITCH US LIKE USUAL IF HE SCORES?
PROBABLY. WHAT DO LADIES SEE IN HIM? HE'S LIKE A TEN YEAR OLD WITH A LIBIDO.
MAYBE THAT'S THE APPEAL.
FUCKED IF I KNOW. ALL I DO KNOW IS ONE PERSON NOT GETTING ANY OF THAT ACTION TONIGHT IS ME.
YOU EVEN GOING TO MAKE AN ATTEMPT?
NAH.
SO WHY ARE YOU HERE?
I WAS GOING TO SAY WHY ARE ANY OF US HERE, BUT THAT SOUNDS LIKE I'M TRYING TO BE PROFOUND IN THE HACKIEST WAY.
BECAUSE I DIDN'T WANT TO BE ALONE DRAWING DICK AND SUPERHEROIC HORSESHOE CRABS.
WELL, I'M AT LEAST TAKING A STAB. GONNA GO GET MY DANCE ON.
YUP. GODSPEED.
AND HERE I AM. THIS IS PROGRESS? LAST TIME I WAS DOING THIS I WAS WITH SYLV, SO I HAD NO HORSE IN THE RACE. NOW I'M JUST ANOTHER SADDO AT THE CLUB.

12:10 A.M.
FUCK IT, THIS PLACE IS DEAD!
ROBBA, HERE, IS "LUCKY PIERRE."
LET'S JUST HIT THE EAST VILLAGE BARS. LESS PRESSURE.
EAST FOURTH, BETWEEN FIRST AND A, PLEASE.
YES, PLEASE.
12:32 A.M.
LEAVE IT TO MAX TO PICK A DUMP. S'FINE, S'FINE.
IT IS PRETTY SEEDY.
YOU LADIES ARE TOO DELICATE. FIRST ROUND'S ON ME IF YOU STOP KVETCHING.
GIMME A CIG. I NEED TO FILTER THE SECONDHAND SMOKE THROUGH SOME OF MY OWN.
I LOVE IT. I ALWAYS ENJOY WATCHING YOU WALK ON THE WILD SIDE.
GIMME ONE, TOO.
OOH, A CIRCLE JERK "ALIVE WITH PLEASURE."
COULD THAT HAVE SOUNDED GAYER?
WHY YOU GOTTA BE SUCH A 'PHOBE, 'PHOBE?
Mets

HEY! I HEAR YOU WAS STARTIN' RUMORS ABOU' THA' GIRL OVER THERE.
HUH? WHAT ARE YOU TALKING ABOUT?
THA' GIRL OVER THERE. YOU'S STARTIN' RUMORS ABOU' HER.
UM, WHAT GIRL? I DON'T EVEN SEE ANY GIRLS IN--
YOU CALLIN' ME A LIAR?
NEW YORK
UM, NO. NOT A LIAR. JUST MISTAKEN. I DON'T KNOW WHAT "GIRL" YOU'RE TALKING ABOUT, BUT WE JUST GOT HERE--
YOU WAS STARTIN' RUMORS--
--AND WE'RE JUST LEAVING. YOU HAVE A GOOD NIGHT, NOW.
NEW YORK
YOU GUYS WERE A BIG HELP.
UH, GARGANTUA'S TWIN WAS STANDING BEHIND YOU GIVING US THE DOUBLE-BARRELED STINK-EYE.
WHAT GIRL WAS HE TALKIN'--
≷SIGH≶ THERE WAS NO GIRL. HE WAS JUST A DRUNK DOUCHE PICKING A FIGHT.
OHHHH. OKAY. MAX IS BARRED FROM BAR-PICKING. I KNOW A PLACE. LOW-KEY, GOOD JUKEBOX.
GORE2000
12:45 A.M.
I CAN LIVE WITH THIS.
FROM KOBS THAT'S A FUCKIN' RAVE. BARKEEP, YOUR FINEST WHITE RUSSIAN FOR MY FINE-ASSED NEWLY DIVORCED CONFRERE. AND YOU, MAXIE?
A ROLLING ROCK.
ALWAYS MUST YOU SHAME ME?

ROUND TWO.
"HERE'S TO GOOD FRIENDS, THE NIGHT IS KINDA SPECIAL..."
ESPECIALLY BECAUSE WE'RE NOT DRINKING LÖWENBRÄU.
SAYS THE MAN DRINKING PIßWASSER.
EXIT
YOU DON'T WANT TO PLAY?
I DON'T WANT TO EMBARRASS MYSELF. I CAN SEE WHY YOU LIKE THE JUKEBOX HERE: ALL BRIT-POP OR BRIT-MOPE.
SORRY THERE'S NO SLAYER FOR KOBS. 'EAVY MEH'UHL, 'EAVY MEH'UHL, MANG!
YOU A SLAYER FAN, BRO? ME TOO. JARED.
UH, ROB?
YEAH, MAN, WHEN WE WAS IN THE SHIT IN KOSOVO WE PUMPED THE SLAYER TO GET US IN A KILLING FRAME OF MIND, DUDE.
OH, UM...
NO DISRESPECT, BRO, BUT YOUR COMPADRES LOOK SOFT. YOU LOOK LIKE YOU SEEN SOME SHIT, AM I RIGHT?
UM, NOT--

I RECOGNIZE "THE LOOK" AND YOU, BRO, HAVE "THE LOOK." I WAS A PARATROOPER. 82ND AIRBORNE. YEAH, I SEEN A LOTTA SHIT, BRO. SHIT YOU CAN'T UN-SEE.
I CAN IMAGINE.
AS CAN YOU. IMAGINE. THAT WAS A U.N. ACTION, WASN'T IT? NATO? CAN'T REMEMBER.
GETTIN' KOBS A REFILL.
1:22 A.M. ROUNDS THREE AND FOUR.
TWO RUSKIES FOR A THIRSTY BOY.
RUSKIES? DON'T LIKE 'EM. RUSSIANS LIKE SLOVADERN MISOLOBICK.
RUSSIAN? SLOBODAN MILOŠEVIĆ? BUT HE--
RED CURTAIN, BRO. ALL THAT ETHNO-CLEANSING, BRO. THE CZECHS WEREN'T KIDDING AROUND.
"RED CURTAIN"? CZECHS? BUT--
DON'T CORRECT HIM.
1:58 A.M.
THAT'S ROUGH, BRO. AN' YOU THINK SHE MAYBE CHEATED ON YOU? DAG. UH--
I NOT SURE AN' I DON' WANNA ASK 'CAUSE THAT'D MEAN TALKIN' T' HER AN' I DON' WANNA DO THAT. SHE'S TROUBLE.
I GOT A GIRLFRIEND, BUT SHE'S IN WINNIPEG.
2:15 A.M. ROUND FIVE.
WHUH TH' HELL'S THIS? WHERE THIS COME FROM? TASTE S'LIKE HAWAIIAN PUTCH.
AN ALABAMA SLAMMER.
HEY! WHERE'D DYLAN KLEBOLD GEDDOFF TO?
(SH-SH-SHHHH. HE'S IN THE BATHROOM. LET'S JUST GO WHILE HE'S IN THERE.)

THA' GUY WAS CREEPY. REAL LIAR-MOUTH COLUMBINE WANNABE. KOSOVO? BUHSHIT. WHA'S HE: TWELVE?!?
HE CALLED US PUSSIES AND ALL HE WAS DRINKING WAS GINGER ALE.
IT IS HI-LARIOUS T' SEE KOBS EL SHITFACED. HOO... THOSE BELGIAN BEERS ARE STRONG, THO'. I MUS'VE DRANK TWELVE. AT LIKE 14% ALCOHOL EACH.
YOU HAD MAYBE SIX. MAYBE. I CALL TWELVE A BIT OF MATT-BELLISHMENT.
OOOOH. OOOOOH. CLEH-VUHHHH. SO CLEVER, MAXIE-BO-BAXIE. GO HOME AND WANK, YOU WANKER.
ENOUGH WI' TH' AN-TAG-ON-ISM.
ADORABLE. SOUND IT OUT, CHAMPERS. HOOKED ON PHONICS.
I SHOULDA PEE 'FORE WE LEFT. I GODDA PEE. LONG TRIP HOME.
RITE OF PASSAGE, DUDE: KOBS IS PLASTERED. KOBS NEEDS TO PEE ON THE STREET. IT'S THE LAW.
I SHOULD HAVE PEED, TOO.
OH, SWEET RELIEF.
SWORD FIGHT? CROSS STREAMS?
NEVER CROSS THE STREAMS!

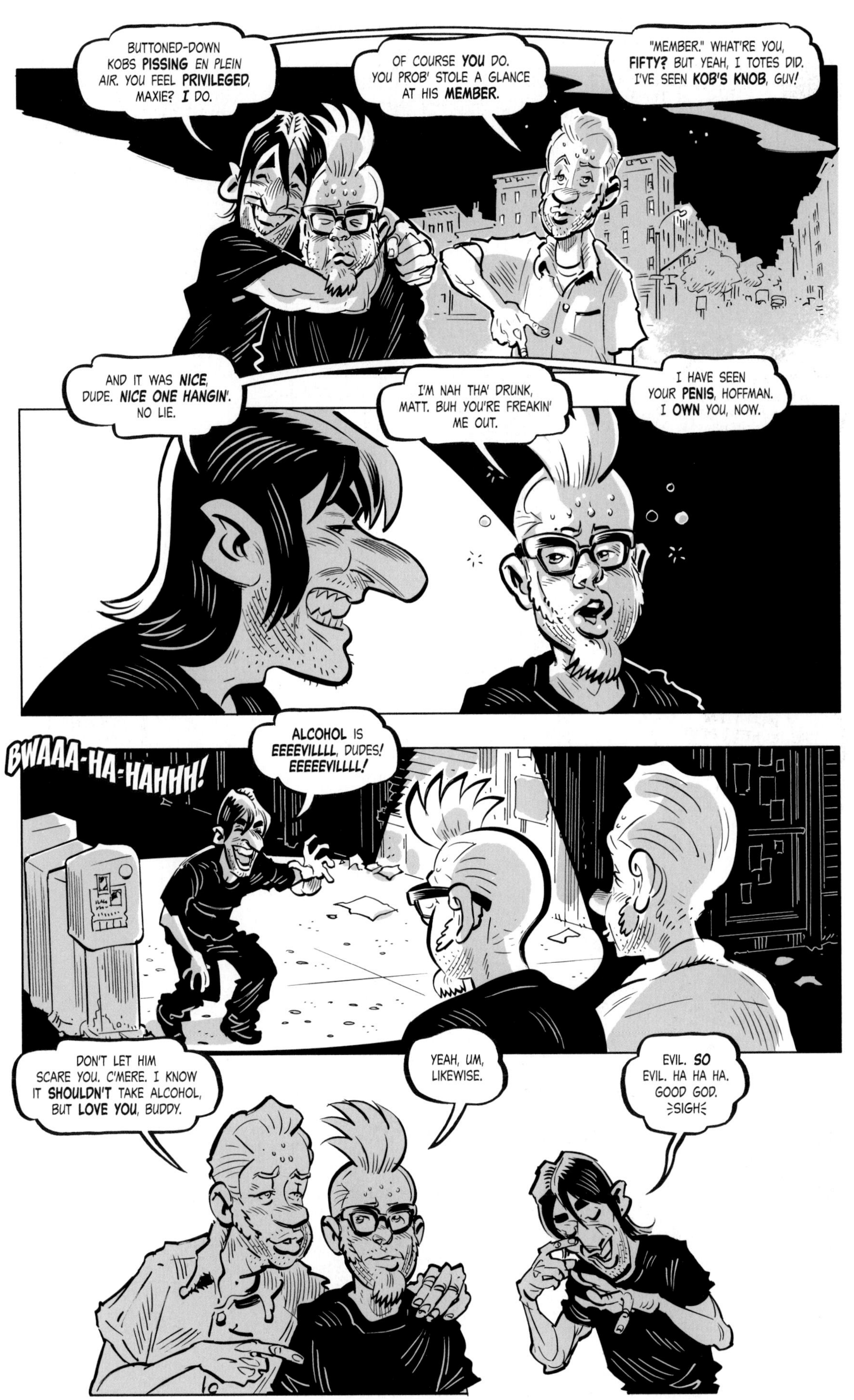
BUTTONED-DOWN KOBS PISSING EN PLEIN AIR. YOU FEEL PRIVILEGED, MAXIE? I DO.
OF COURSE YOU DO. YOU PROB' STOLE A GLANCE AT HIS MEMBER.
"MEMBER." WHAT'RE YOU, FIFTY? BUT YEAH, I TOTES DID. I'VE SEEN KOB'S KNOB, GUV!
AND IT WAS NICE, DUDE. NICE ONE HANGIN'. NO LIE.
I'M NAH THA' DRUNK, MATT. BUH YOU'RE FREAKIN' ME OUT.
I HAVE SEEN YOUR PENIS, HOFFMAN. I OWN YOU, NOW.
BWAAA-HA-HAHHH!
ALCOHOL IS EEEEVILLLL, DUDES! EEEEEVILLLL!
DON'T LET HIM SCARE YOU. C'MERE. I KNOW IT SHOULDN'T TAKE ALCOHOL, BUT LOVE YOU, BUDDY.
YEAH, UM, LIKEWISE.
EVIL. SO EVIL. HA HA HA. GOOD GOD. ≶SIGH≶

2:54 A.M.
SO, AROUND OR THROUGH WASHINGTON SQUARE?
DON'T BE A FUCKIN' PUSSY. THROUGH. GO THROUGH.
OH, HEY: TAXI!!!
7H35
NYC TAXI 7H35
LATER, QUEENS-PEASANT SCUM! HAPPY TRAILS FOR YOUR HAPPY TRAILS!
SOMETIMES I DO NOT LIKE THAT GUY.
SO, AROUND OR THROUGH?
THROUGH S'QUICKER.
7H35
YO, SMOKE. SMOKE.
YO, SINSE. SINSE.
I THOUGHT GIULIANI CLEARED OUT ALL THE DEALERS.
WHUHYUH THINK HE IS, BATMAN?
OOF. THA' SLAMMA BAMMER DIDDA NUMBER ON ME. ZHEEZUS. WHY WE ALLUS HIT THE EAS' VILLAGE? ISSA SHITHOLE.
YO, SMOKE. SMOKE.
YO, SINSE. SINSE.

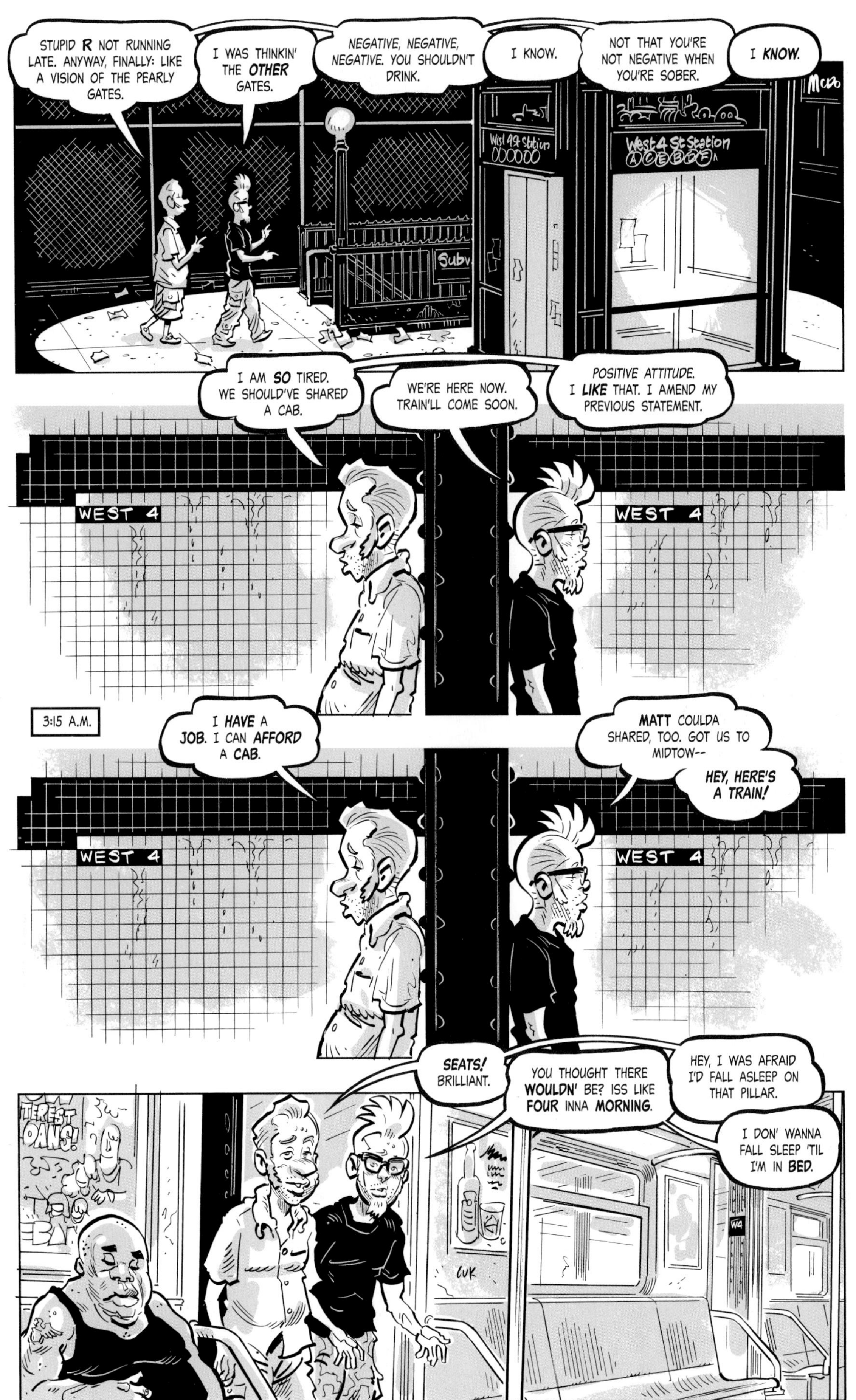
STUPID **R** NOT RUNNING LATE. ANYWAY, FINALLY: LIKE A VISION OF THE PEARLY GATES.
I WAS THINKIN' THE ***OTHER*** GATES.
NEGATIVE, NEGATIVE, NEGATIVE. YOU SHOULDN'T DRINK.
I KNOW.
NOT THAT YOU'RE NOT NEGATIVE WHEN YOU'RE SOBER.
I ***KNOW.***
West 4 St Station
Subw
I AM **SO** TIRED. WE SHOULD'VE SHARED A CAB.
WE'RE HERE NOW. TRAIN'LL COME SOON.
POSITIVE ATTITUDE. I ***LIKE*** THAT. I AMEND MY PREVIOUS STATEMENT.
WEST 4
WEST 4
3:15 A.M.
I ***HAVE*** A **JOB**. I CAN ***AFFORD*** A **CAB**.
MATT COULDA SHARED, TOO. GOT US TO MIDTOW--
HEY, HERE'S A TRAIN!
WEST 4
WEST 4
SEATS! BRILLIANT.
YOU THOUGHT THERE ***WOULDN'*** BE? ISS LIKE **FOUR** INNA **MORNING**.
HEY, I WAS AFRAID I'D FALL ASLEEP ON THAT PILLAR.
I DON' WANNA FALL SLEEP 'TIL I'M IN **BED**.

4:12 A.M.
71ST AND CONTINENTAL. NEXT STOP--
OHSHITOHSHITOHSHIT, WE GOTTA GET OFF!
YEESH, LOCAL'S NOT RUNNING EITHER DIRECTION. I'M TAKING A CAB.
'SUMIN' THERE ARE ANY.
GOOD POINT. THIS TIME O' NIGHT. MORNING. WHICHEVER. I DON'T WANNA WALK.
71 Continental Avenue
NO CABS. FUCK. I JUST WANNA BE IN BED BEFORE SUNRISE.
ME TOO. COUPLA DRACULAS. GODDA 'BOUT 'N HOUR 'FORE SUN-UP.
THIS IS THE BATAAN DEATH MARCH OF TRIPS HOME.
NODDA WAX HYPERBOLIC.
HEAVEN FORFEND.

IT WAS REAL.
REAL LONG AN' DRAWN OUT. LIKE THIS HAN'SHAKE I TOO DRUNK FOR.
DRINK WATER BEFORE YOU TURN IN OR YOU'LL GET A HANGOVER.
OKAY. THANKS. G'NIGHT.
G'MORNING.
4:44 A.M.
77-12
I ALLUS THOUGHT "THE SPINS" WAS A MYTH, BUT ZHEEZUSS...
SOCIAL DRINK, MAYBE. MAYBE. LONELY DRINK, NEVER AGAIN.
SHIT: FORGOT TO DRINK WATER. OR BRUSH MY TEETH. I DON' WANNA--
ZZZZZZZZZZZZZZ

TUESDAY, JULY 18TH, 12:25 P.M.

1:45 P.M.
YOU KNOW IT'S AIR CONDITIONED INDOORS, RIGHT? OR DO YOU JUST LIKE SOOT AND SWEAT IN YOUR FOOD?
NOT A BIG FAN OF A.C. MAYBE IT'S THE DESERT IN MY BLOOD.
LIKE YOU'VE EVER EVEN BEEN TO ISRAEL.
I CHOOSE TO HONOR MY PARENTS' DECISION TO GET THE HECK OUT OF THERE.
French Roast
SO IT'S OFFICIAL: YOU'RE DIVORCED. UM, CONGRATULATIONS?
THANKS? YEAH, WHAT'S THE ETIQUETTE?
THE ETIQUETTE IS THAT OCEAN OF LADIES ROLLING ON BY IS NOW YOURS TO SWIM IN.
YOU KNOW I DON'T KNOW HOW TO SWIM.
LITERALIST. YOU'VE BEEN DOING ALL RIGHT FOR YOURSELF, EVEN WITH THE FLOATIES.
THAT YOUR LATEST EPITHET FOR CONDOMS?
NO, BUT THAT'S NOT BAD. ANYWAY, YOU'VE BEEN PLENTY "BUSY."
PFF
YOU'RE GREEDY. YOU WANT EMOTIONAL CONNECTION. YOU ARE ON THE REBOUND. YOU'RE A TERRIBLE PROSPECT. JUST FUCK.
NOW LET ME EAT MY SANDWICH. IT'S MY ONLY ORAL--
UCCH, STOP. JUST PUT IT IN YOUR MOUTH.

LOOK AT YOU MOPPING YOUR BROW FROM ALL THESE FREE-RANGE NUBILES.
I'M MOPPING 'COS IT'S LIKE A HUNDRED DEGREES.
YOU SHOULD SCHTUP DEPUTY DEEDEE AGAIN. WHO CARES SHE'S MARRIED? WHO CARES SHE'S FIFTY-WHATEVER? DO IT.
YOU'RE A REAL ROMANTIC.
JUST. DO. IT.
8:40 P.M.
I'M DELIGHTED YOU RANG, THOUGH I CONFESS A TRIFLE SURPRISED. I THOUGHT I'D SEEN THE LAST OF YOU.
OH, HEH. I WAS JUST A LITTLE OVER-WHELMED. THE WHOLE MARRIED THING.
SPEAKING OF WHICH, MY DIVORCE PAPERS CAME TODAY.
AH, SO THERE'S THE RUB. THE DIVORCE IS FINALIZED AND YOU SEEK SOLACE FROM--
NO, NO. I JUST WANTED TO--
ACTUALLY, MY FRIEND JACK SAID I SHOULD CALL YOU AGAIN.
SAGACIOUS FRIEND. IS HE ATTRACTIVE? ADVENTUROUS? PERHAPS HE'D LIKE TO JOIN--
NO, NO. NO. NOPE. NO, HE'S A REAL PRUDE. PRACTICALLY A QUAKER--

SO THEN: HERE'S THE RUB. OH MY, A SMIDGE PIQUANT.
JEEZ, SORRY. IT'S SO HOT OUT. I SHOULD GO FRESHEN--
I WOULDN'T HEAR OF IT. YOU'VE BEEN MARINATING AND I AM A GOURMAND. MM. BRINY. MMMM--
OH YES, THAT'S THE BUSINESS.
UH, CONDOM?
PET, THIS ISN'T THE BEST PILLOW TALK, BUT I WENT THROUGH MENOPAUSE YEARS AGO. NO BABIES, NO S.T.D.s.
DEAR BOY, YOUR EYES HAVE NOT LEFT THE DOOR.
I'VE SEEN TOO MANY PLAYBOY CARTOONS--
AH, "MY WIFE, MY BEST FRIEND." LET'S REPAIR TO THE BOUDOIR.
10:24 P.M.
TO PARAPHRASE J.F.K., THAT WAS THE VIGOR I NEEDED.
I STILL CAN'T HELP BUT PICTURE YOUR HUSBAND BARGING IN, DRESSED LIKE ALLAN QUATERMAIN.
HAH! I SHOULD BE SO LUCKY. EVEN WERE HE TO APPEAR, THE MOST HE'D MANAGE WOULD BE A MILDLY REBUKING HARRUMPH. HE'D THEN RETIRE TO THE LIVING ROOM TO SULK IN A SNIFTER OF COGNAC.

STAY THE NIGHT? I'D **SO** ENJOY A WARM BODY BESIDE ME IN THIS LARGE BED.
I'VE GOT A--
SURE, *OF COURSE*. EXCUSE ME FOR A MOMENT. I NEED TO FRESHEN UP, FOR **REAL** THIS TIME.
(HI MOM. I WAS JUST CALLING TO SAY I WON'T BE HOME TO--
OH JEEZ, FORCE OF HABIT. I TOTALLY SPACED I HAVE MY ***OWN*** *PLACE NOW. I'M SORRY.*
YEAH. HEH. NO. SORRY. RIGHT, YOU TRAINED ME WELL. ***TOO*** *WELL. HA. OKAY, LOVE YOU. BYE.)*
A CALL TO MOTHER?
OMIGOD, I'M **SO** EMBARRASSED.
IT'S REALLY VERY SWEET. ALMOST **TOO** SWEET. AS IF I'VE JUST BEEN SERVICED BY A SWEET LITTLE BOY.
I SUPPOSE IT'S FITTING DEPUTY DEEDEE SLEEPS LOOKING LIKE *THE LONE RANGER*.
WHAT THE **HELL** AM I *DOING?* THIS IS JUST WHAT JACK SAID: A PORT IN THE STORM.
ALL I DO IS ASSESS **EVERY** FEMALE I SEE. **NONSTOP**. THEIR ***FUCKABILITY QUOTIENT***. CHECKLISTS.
PLEASE **SLEEP**, YOU ***JERK***. PLEASE. FOR THE LOVE OF GOD ***JUST SHUT THE FUCK UP*** AND SLEEP. ***SLEEP!***
BRAIN TO ROB: **NO**.

THURSDAY, JULY 20TH, 2:36 P.M.
I LOVE IT: YOU ACTUALLY FOLLOWED MY SUGGESTION. YOU ARE A DOG. A LUCKY DOG. JEEZ, DEPUTY DEEDEE IS A LIBERTINE.
YEAH. UH, I HAVEN'T TOLD HER YET, BUT I'M DONE. I LIKE HER BUT IT DOESN'T FEEL RIGHT. THE MARRIED THING, THE AGE THING--
DONE?!? IT'S THE AGE THING, ISN'T IT? YOU SUPERFICIAL--
IT'S THE MARRIED THING. EVEN IF DUSTY NOODLE IS OFF IN WHOKNOWSWHEREISTAN SORTING RELICS, HE'S STILL HER HUSBAND.
GRAY'S PAPAYA
GRAY'S PAPAYA
AH. SPOKEN LIKE A MAN WHOSE OWN WIFE--
LET'S LEAVE THAT THOUGHT UNFINISHED.
WELL, IF SHE'S LOOKING FOR SOMEONE A LITTLE LESS BURDENED BY CONSCIENCE BUT A LOT MORE BURDENED BY CYAN TESTES--
YOU KNOW WHAT? THAT'S NOT A BAD IDEA.
I KNEW YOU WOULDN'T--
WAIT, WHAT? YOU'D DO THAT?
WE COULD DO BRUNCH. SHE LOVES THIS STODGY FRENCH JOINT WHERE ALL THE OTHER PATRONS CUT THEIR FOOD WITH STONE TOOLS. FROM THEIR CHILDHOODS. BECAUSE THEY'RE OLD.
YEAH, I GOT THAT.

YOU DO THIS FOR ME AND ALL YOUR DEBTS ARE FORGIVEN.
I DON'T OWE YOU ANYTHING.
ANY YOU NEVER WILL, SON. YOU NEVER WILL. OMIGOD, I'M PRACTICALLY PRE'-ING.
GLAD I FINISHED MY WIENER BEFORE YOU PLANTED THE IMAGE OF YOUR DRIPPY ONE IN MY BRAIN.
SO WHAT NEXT FOR YOU: MORE PROFILES ON S'LOVE?
NAH. I CAN'T DEAL WITH THE ADDED ELEMENT OF REJECTION. BUT I'M STILL GETTING HITS.
YOU SURE YOU WANT ME TO TRY TO SET YOU UP WITH DEEDEE?
ABSOLUTELY. GIRLS OUR AGE HAVE NO INTEREST IN ME. IT TAKES AN OLDER WOMAN TO APPRECIATE WHAT I HAVE TO OFFER.
KYUSS
ANYHOO, GOTTA GO. THE GATEFOLD AWAITS.
THE ONE YOU'RE PAINTING OR THE ONE YOU'RE GONNA WHACK IT TO?
YOU SAY THAT AS IF THERE'S A DIFFERENCE. KIDDING. DUTY CALLS.
SOMEHOW THAT DOESN'T ANSWER MY QUESTION.
SALE!
YUP. YUP. TOTALLY. OF COURSE. OH MY YES. YUP. TOTALLY. YES, OF COURSE. OMIGOD.

JUST STOP IT. JESUS CHRIST, WITH THE ASSESSING, ASSESSING, ASSESSING. STOP COMMODIFYING BODY PARTS.
THIS ONE HAS A PERFECT ASS. THIS ONE HAS PERFECT TITS. THIS ONE A PERFECT MIDRIFF. THIS ONE--
HOPELESS. I'M IN MY OWN HEAD AND I FIND ME AN UNSYMPATHETIC CHARACTER.
THAT ONE TOTALLY HAD THE PERFECT ONION BOOTY, THOUGH. WOW.
GODDAM LIBIDO.
1:27 A.M.
MAYBE I SHOULD LOOK AT SOME OTHER PROFILES. WINNOW IT DOWN TO THE SAME LIKES AND DISLIKES SO I CAN END UP DATING ME WITH TITS. UGH.
IS THERE AN OPPOSITES ATTRACT DOT COM? IS THAT A MILLION DOLLAR IDEA OR THE STUPIDEST FUCKING THING EVER?
S'LOVE
ACTUALLY, THIS ONE, NEKTARBAD, SOUNDS GOOD. "RIBALD." "JEWISH BUT NOT RELIGIOUS." I CAN WORK WITH THAT.
ARTSY PIC CROPPED TO JUST THE EYES MIGHT BE A RED FLAG. SEXY EYES, THO'. I'LL SEND A SUBMISSION. RESPONSE. WHATEVER, THEN BACK TO THE HORSESHOE CRABS.
S'LOVE
NEKTARBAD
I SHOULD SIMPLIFY MY STYLE OR I MIGHT BLOW MY DEADLINE. IT'S NOT LIKE I'M DOING GROOVY PRIX, I'M DOING LICENSED PRIX. FOR KIDDIEWINKS.

LITTLE EARLY TO BE PHONING IT IN, AIN'T IT, HOSS?
HUH? I'M NOT--
YOU WAS SAYIN' YOU CAN SIMPLIFY. THAT'S FANCY TALK FOR CUTTIN' CORNERS!
ART IS BEST SERVED BY BEING REDUCTIVE. ECONOMY OF LINE. LOOK AT HIRSCHFELD. YOUR NAMESAKES--
OH JEEZ, NOW HE'S BRINGIN' IN TH' NAMESAKES THING. FINE, PRIX SOUND OFF:
DUCHAMP!
GROSZ!
ARP!
SCHWITTERS!
AND THESE HIGHFALUTIN NAMESAKES--
--WERE THE RESULT OF BEING BAKED IN ART HISTORY CLASS.
WHAT'S FUNNIER THAN DADA, DUDE?
OUR CREATORS NEVER THOUGHT THIS HYPERVIOLENT COMIC WOULD END UP A MARKETING JUGGERNAUT. FOR KIDS!
CECI N'EST PAS UNE PIPE.
THAT'S MAGRITTE.
TRUE. BUT YOU'RE DREAMING THIS AND YOU DON'T KNOW ANY DUCHAMP QUOTES.
CHIPS
Ceci n'est pas une p.p.
APROPOS: YOUR WORK HAS GONE FROM THE GUTTER TO THE SEWER.
SYLVIA?!? WHAT ARE YOU DOING HERE?
I'M ALWAYS HERE, ROB. ALWAYS. TICKING AWAY IN THE BACK OF YOUR MIND. "DID I DO THE RIGHT THING? DID I? DID I?"

BANG AS MANY HAGGISH CHILDHOOD CRUSHES AS YOU WANT. AS MANY STONER BLONDES AND SO ON, BUT IT'S ALWAYS ME YOUR MIND COMES BACK TO.
NO FLIMSY CERTIFICATE OF DIVORCE IS GONNA EXORCISE ME FROM YOUR FRAGILE, TORMENTED PSYCHE. YOU POOR--
PLEASE--
WE'VE GOT YOUR BACK, ROB-SAN!
PRIX ASSEMBLE! DEFENSE POSITIONS!
THIS IS JUST SAD. IT'S A DREAM. YOU COULD BE BONING ME AND INSTEAD YOUR STUPID VAGUELY PHALLIC WORK-FOR-HIRE STOOGES COCKBLOCK YOU. PAGING DR. FREUD.
SHE MAKES A SOLID POINT. PRIX, RETREAT.
A NO-PANTS DREAM, YOUR EX IN SEXY GEAR AND NOTHING. NO ACTION. I HOPE THE COLORIST USES LOTS OF BLUE DOWN THERE.
AND UP HERE. BECAUSE YOU'RE BLUE, PET. VERY, VERY BLUE.

5:36 A.M.
PREDAWN WITH A RAGING **PEE-BONER**, COURTESY OF DREAM SYLVIA.
OH C'MON, **GET SOFT**. THIS IS **RIDICULOUS**. ALMOST AS RIDICULOUS AS SCOLDING MY OWN ANATOMY.
DREAM SYLVIA LANDED A FEW SOLID SHOTS. BUT IT'S **YOUR** BRAIN, **IDIOT**. YOUR SCRIPT. JUST **YOU**.
I'VE NEVER LIVED **ALONE**. THAT'S GOTTA BE IT. MOM, THEN JACK, THEN SYLV, THEN MOM AGAIN. NOW *THIS*. ME ALONE WITH MY TOXIC THOUGHTS.
FRITZ
AND THESE DIVORCE PAPERS.
OKAY. LET'S CHECK SOME EMAIL. ANOTHER HIT ON MY PROFILE. **DARK-PHANTASI**. LIKE A *GOTHY OSMOND*. LOTTA TEETH, BUT CUTE. SHE AND NEKTARBAD--
ZZZZZZZZZZ...

SATURDAY, JULY 22ND, NOONISH.
JEEZ, ROBBIE, NO OFFENSE, BUT YOU LOOK LIKE **SHIT**.
HOW COULD I **POSSIBLY** TAKE OFFENSE? I HAVEN'T BEEN SLEEPING WELL.
CAR INSURANCE
INSTANT Tax Service
TOWER DINER
NEPHEW ART
SIGN PAINTING
IT'S BEING ALONE WITH NOTHING BUT HORSESHOE CRABS, DIVORCE PAPERS AND MY OWN THOUGHTS TO KEEP ME COMPANY.
DARK CIRCLES UNDER YOUR EYES. THROW ON A LITTLE **MASCARA** AND YOU'RE **GOTH**.
I'M TRYING TO THINK IF I'VE EVER LIVED ALONE. NOPE. ALWAYS ROOMMATES OR FAMILY AROUND.
YEAH. NOT SO FUNNY ***NOW***, IS IT? YOU **THINK** IT'S GONNA BE LIBERATING, BUT...
GIVE IT TIME. HAVE YOU ACTUALLY BROUGHT A **FEMALE** BACK THERE YET? **THAT'LL** MAKE ***ALL*** THE DIFF'.
I HAVE SOME MORE PROSPECTS ON S'LOVE. INCLUDING A GOTH.
AH. YOU'VE DONE ALL RIGHT. WHAT'S YOUR SECRET? ARE YOU A BIG OL' LIAR?
HILARIOUS. I DUNNO. I MUST GO INTO SOME FUGUE STATE 'COS CLEARLY I WRITE GOOD SHIT BUT CAN'T RECALL DOING IT.
BUT REMEMBER: I'VE ONLY ACTUALLY "DATED" ONE GIRL AND IT DIDN'T WORK OUT, SOOOO...

WEDNESDAY, JULY 26TH, 12:45 P.M.
ON THE STARBUCKS MERRY-GO-ROUND AGAIN. JESUS. I HOPE THIS ONE IS--
OH SHIT: IT'S SHEILA. GOD, THIS ISN'T EXACTLY NEAR GANDER. FUCK. HOW EMBARRASSING.
CLUNGE!
RAAAHHHB. WHAT ARE YOU DOING HERE STANDING AROUND IN THE HEAT?
UH, JUST MEETING SOMEONE. DON'T LET ME SLOW YOU DOWN.
YOU'RE NOT. I'M, UH. NO. BUT MAYBE YEAH. SHITBALLS, FOR REALS? UH, "FILDICKIAN"?
OH LORD, REALLY?
"NEKTARBAD"?
M50
YOU'RE MARRIED. YOU EXPRESSLY TOLD ME--
YOU SEE A RING, SHERLOCK? I TELL COWORKERS THAT TO AVOID MESSINESS. BECAUSE, AS NOTED, GANDER'S A HOTSPOT OF INAPPROPRIATENESS.
BUT YOU'RE THE REIGNING QUEEN OF THAT SHIT.
TRUE DAT, AND WHAT BETTER RUSE THAN A NONEXISTENT HUBBY?
GODFLESH
SO WHATTA WE DO? GO OUR SEPARATE WAYS AND PRETEND THIS DIDN'T HAPPEN?
GAY. I SAY GO WITH IT AND KEEP IT SECRET AT GANDER. SNEAKY-STYLEE.
I'VE CAUGHT YOU STEALING GLANCES AT MY HEINIE AND CLEAVAGE.
LOOKA: LIFE IS NOTHING BUT ONE CLICHE CHASING ANOTHER, WRAPPED IN COINCIDENCE.

I WROTE SOME SHIT THAT SNAGGED YOUR EYES AND VICE VERSA. I MEAN, "FILDICKIAN"? I SHOULDA KNOWN.
WHAT CAN I SAY? I LIKE ME SOME DICK.
DOES THAT JOKE EVER GET OLD? ASSUMING IT IS A JOKE AND DOING WORK FOR ME HASN'T BROUGHT YOU OVER TO THE DICK SIDE.
I LOVE PHILIP K. DICK. I DIDN'T NAME HIM. I JUST LOVE CAPITAL D DICK.
GODFLESH
YIKES, IZZAT TH' TIME? GOTTA GET BACK. SO, DOES THE SECRET SEX LIFE OF WALTER MITTY BEGIN OR WHAT?
I ACTUALLY CAUTIONED MYSELF NOT TO ASK YOU OUT. BEFORE I EVEN KNEW YOU WERE MARRIED, WHICH NOW--
YEAH, YEAH. CAT, BAG, OUT. WE DOING THIS?
OH YEAH, WE'RE DOING THIS. WE ARE SO DOING THIS.
FUCK YEAH, WE ARE. NOT ALL YOU GUYS THAT DRAW THE DIRTY KNOW HOW TO DO THE DIRTY, BUT YOU ARE METHOD, BABY. METHOD!
BWOWNT-BWOWNT-
WHA--
CELLPHONE. ON VIBRATE. IGNORE IT.
BWOWNT-BWOWNT-
BUT--
SERIOUSLY. IGNORE IT. FUCKING.

I WAS RIGHT: YOUR DONG DOES LOOK LIKE THE ONES YOU DRAW. I KNEW IT. ALL YOU GUYS--
GROUND RULE: NO CHAT ABOUT OTHER GUYS' DONGS. I DON'T WANNA KNOW.
OKAY. AND I DON'T WANNA KNOW FROM STRAY VADGE.
WHO CALLED WHILE WE WERE AT IT, BY THE WAY? WAS IT A GIRL? IT WAS A GIRL, WASN'T IT? WASN'T IT?!?
KIDDING.
THERE'S PLENTY ROOM FOR BIG FUN BETWEEN US. NOTHING TOO SERIOUS, CHECK? NO STRINGS. BUT COVERT IS THE GOLDEN RULE. IF THEM JACKALS--
MUM'S THE WORD.
OH, THAT'S RULE NUMBA TWO: NO "P" WORD.
UH, PUSS--?
EEEE? HELP ME OUT.
"PUSSY" IS FINE. UNDIES, CHECK. KNICKERS, MAYBE. FRILLIES, IF THEY ARE. P-A-N-T-I-E-S, UH-UH. GROSS.
GOT ANYTHING TO EAT OR ARE YOU ONE OF THOSE JAR OF MAYO IN THE FRIDGE GUYS?
MMMM, JESUS. COLD SESAME NOODLES. YOU TH' BOMB. THANKS FOR THE SHIRT. I CAN'T EAT TOPLESS.
BUT BOTTOM-LESS IS OKAY.
LESS CHANCE OF FOOD DRIPPING UP MY COOCH THAN ON THE TWINS. GOD, WORKING AT GANDER HAS FUCKIN' RUINED ME. I USED TO BE A NICE GIRL. A TERRIBLE UPTIGHT LAY, BUT NICE.

3:47 A.M.
SHE'S TOTALLY RIGHT: I DO DRAW MY OWN DICK. JEEZ.
OH, WHO DID CALL BEFORE?
DARLING, THIS IS DEEDEE. I'VE BEEN CONSIDERING YOUR CHEEKY PROPOSITION, RE PIMPING YOUR FRIEND OUT TO ME. OR IS IT ME YOU'RE PIMPING TO YOUR FRIEND? SORRY SO COARSE, BUT I'M INTRIGUED.
GOOD LORD, YOUR PROVINCIAL MORES MUST BE AT CONSTANT ODDS WITH YOUR PORNOGRAPHIC ENDEAVORS. REGARDLESS, SWEET, DO CALL AND LET'S DISCUSS.
MY GOD IF I HAD A HUSBAND WHOSE ANATOMY WAS WORTH A--
CLICK
JACK WILL BE OVER THE MOON.
THURSDAY, JULY 27TH, 8:30 A.M.
IT WAS NICE, HOFFMAN. NICE. ESPECIALLY THOSE SESAME NOODLES. KIDDING. IT WAS ALL GOOD.
AND CHECK THIS: HANDING IN YOUR ASSIGNMENTS AS I HEAD IN--
MILK
CIGARS
--WEARING THE SAME CLOTHES LIKE THOSE GOONS WILL EVEN NOTICE. NOT.
DID YOU STAY UP ALL NIGHT DOING THIS? I'M LIKE SAWING LOGS AND YOU'RE UP DRAWING COCK FOR ME?
YEAH. COULDN'T SLEEP. I'LL GET SOME REST NOW.
YOU BETTER. DON'T BRING OUT THE JEWISH MOTHER IN ME. MY MOTHER. YOU DON'T WANT THAT, TRUST ME.
GET SOME FUCKING REST. GIMME KISS.

THIS IS EITHER GOING TO WORK OUT SPLENDIDLY OR BLOW UP SPECTACULARLY.
ATM MACHINE
SAND
Sabbath
TURN IN NOW AND I'M 'ONNA SLEEP 'TIL EVENING. CAFFEINE UP AND GET T' MY PRIX.
DONUT HAVEN
OKAY, SO SAMMY KNOWS MAX AND BRIAN, SO I CAN'T TELL THEM ABOUT SHEILA. JEEZ, THIS REALLY IS ON THE D.L..
24 MINI MART
DOES THE CLANDESTINE THING MAKE IT SEXIER OR JUST MORE WORK? COULD I TELL JACK?
JACK!

I KNOW IT'S EARLY, BUT PICK UP. PICK UP. JACK!
HEY, GOOD MORNING, BUDDY. YEAH, SO...
NO, I WAS UP. REALLY. SHE WHAT?!? REALLY? REALLY? THAT DOES SURPRISE ME. NO, OF COURSE IN A GOOD WAY.
IS TRUE
CORDS AND TAPES
HONEST, I'VE BARELY GIVEN IT A THOUGHT SINCE WE DISCUSSED IT. I DIDN'T ACTUALLY THINK YOU'D DO IT.
...BUT GOSH, RANGER RIVERS, WON'T THAT JUST CONFUSE THE JUNIOR RANGERTEERS?
WELL, SHUCKS, DEPUTY DEEDEE, I THINK THEY CAN RUN WITH IT!
YOU LIAR, I CAN HEAR THE TV IN THE BACKGROUND. NO, I'M SURE IT'S ALL VERY INNOCENT. I'LL SET IT UP. 'KAY. BUH-BYE.
DON'T GIMME THAT LOOK. THIS IS A GOOD THING I'M DOING. JUNIOR RANGERTEERS LOOK OUT FOR ONE ANOTHER.

THAT COFFEE DID **NADA**.
I DUH WANNA SLEEP ALL DAY. SET TH' 'LARM FOR THREE. THA'S NAH S'BAD. PRIX D'SERVE MY FULL--
ZZZZZZZZZZZZZ
YES, ***SLEEP.*** YOU ***FORGOT*** TO PULL THE PIN ON THE ***ALARM*** SO WE HAVE ***ALL DAY*** TOGETHER. ***HERE. YOUR BRAIN, MY WORLD, MY RULES.***

FRIDAY, AUGUST 11TH, 12:20 A.M.
YEESH, BARE ASS AND SOME SKINLESS CG BACON BITS ASIDE, HOLLOW MAN WAS A HUGE PILE OF SHIT.
IT WAS NO TOTAL RECALL.
OR ROBOCOCK. WHATEVUH. NO CELEB FRAME-GRABBING TO WRANGLE FOR THE MAG, AT LEAST.
ALWAYS WORKING.
LINCOLN SQUARE
HOLLOW MAN
PHONE
I KNOW, RIGHT? BUT AFTER WILD THINGS I GET TO EXPENSE MY BACON VIEWING. NOW THAT FLICK--
I DON'T WANT TO DISCUSS BACON'S BUSINESS.
YOU PUT THE "MENTAL" IN COMPARTMENTALIZE. HOW CAN YOU DRAW SUCH FILTH BUT BE SO UPTIGHT? I'M KIDDING.
MY EX--
NEVER MIND.
LET'S HIT THE DINER. I NEED A B.L.T. OR SOMETHING.
YOU'VE GOT BACON ON THE BRAIN.
LUCKY FOR YOU.
JAPANESE RESTAURANT

W 69 ST
West Side RESTAURANT
FREE DELIVERY
OH SWEET MOTHER OF FUCK IS THERE ANYTHING BETTER THAN BACON? GOD. DAMN.
NOT ONE, BUT TWO B.L.T.S. REALLY RUBBING IT IN.
I'LL RUB YOU IN -- AND I WILL, TOO. YOU WILL BE RUBBED, THE RIGHT WAY, I MIGHT ADD. CHRIST I'M A FUCKING AWFUL JEW.
MY EX--
I LOVE A WOMAN THAT CAN ACTUALLY EAT AND ENJOY IT.
DID YOU JUST SAY YOU LOVE ME? OMIGOD, IS THAT WHAT THAT WAS?
I--
OMIGOD YOU ARE SO EASY TO FUCK WITH. I LOVE IT! YOU LOOKED TERRIFIED. IT'S WEIRD 'COS YOU'RE A FUNNY GUY BUT SOMETIMES YOU SEEM SO FUCKING EARNEST.
YOU'RE THE SECOND WOMAN TO ACCUSE ME OF THAT RECENTLY.
REALLY? SO WHO IS THIS CUNT? AND HOW RECENT WE TALKIN' HERE?
IF I HAVE TO TELL YOU I'M KIDDING ONE MORE TIME I'M GONNA START CALLING YOU ERNEST TAKES THE SHORT BUS.
SMEK
YOU'RE A MENACE. YOU'RE GONNA GIVE ME A STROKE.

--KEEP STROKING LIKE THAT.
I'M A MENACE, HUH? A MENACE? HOW MENACING IS THIS?
OH-- UH-- I--
WAIT, THE DUVET--
OH-- MY-- GOD. I NEVER CAME FROM A HANDIE BEFORE.
WHAT KINDA FARCHADAT TEENS DID YOU HAVE?
THE KIND THAT INVOLVED HANDJOBS ONLY FROM MYSELF.
THAT IS TRAGIC. AS IS YOUR MESS ON MY DUVET I SHOULD HAVE REMOVED FROM THE BED SO IT'S MY FAULT REALLY I'M DEFLECTING BLAME SORRY.
CAN YOU IMAGINE THE AMOUNT OF CUM DRY CLEANERS EXPUNGE FROM FINE LINENS? FROM JUST THIS APARTMENT ALONE--
YOU DON'T HAVE TO SAY "I'M KIDDING."
OH DON'T I? MAYBE I DO. MAYBE I COLLECT IT IN JARS. MAYBE I'M THE HOWARD HUGHES OF JIZZ.
IF YOU WEREN'T MOPPING IT OFF WITH A TEE-SHIRT I MIGHT'VE BOUGHT THAT.
I LIKE YOU, HOFFMAN.
I LIKE YOU, WEIST.
UCCH, THE NAME. SHEILA WEIST. THEY USED TO CALL ME SHE'S-A-BEAST OR WILDEBEEST OR--
LET'S HIT THE SHOWER. I DON'T LIKE GOING TO SLEEP SWEATY AND JIZZY.

OH RELAX, I'M JUST PEEING. YOU WERE MARRIED. TO AN ITALIAN. YOU CAN'T BE THIS UPTIGHT.
I'M NOT--
PLEASE. YOU'RE THE UPTIGHTEST GUY EVERYWHERE BUT IN BED. ONCE YOUR DICK IS OUT IT'S LIKE YOU'RE A DIFFERENT GUY. MR. HYDE--
--THE-SALAMI.
IT'S OUT NOW.
YEAH. BUT THE CRAZY JUICE IS DRAINED. ALL OVER MY DUVET. KIDDING.
NO OFFENSE, BUT HOW DO YOU AFFORD THIS PLACE? GANDER CAN'T--
THIS TINY PLACE WITH THIS TOTALLY CRAPPY STALL SHOWER AND NO TUB? MY PARENTS BOUGHT THE BUILDING YEARS AGO. I'M THE ONLY ONE PAYING LIKE NOTHING RENT.
I'M GRATEFUL, MA, I'M GRATEFUL.
SO, YOU UP FOR SECONDS?
SATURDAY, AUGUST 12TH, NOONISH.
I CAN'T BELIEVE YOU'RE DITCHING ME TO GO DRAW FUCKING TRAYF KUNG-FU SHELLFISH.
BELIEVE ME, I'D MUCH RATHER STAY WITH YOU.
IT'S OKAY. MY COOCH NEEDS A REST. PLUS, I GOT ERRANDS UP THE YIN YANG. BUT CALL ME, A'RIGHT?
ONE WAY
Y'S PAPAYA
W 72 ST
BROADWAY
AND HERE I AM WITH MY DICK IN MY HAND IN PUBLIC.
NOPE, NEVER GETS OLD.
72 St
PHILIP K. DICK
CLANS OF THE ALPHANE MOON

SUNDAY, AUGUST 13TH, 1:15 P.M.
...EVERYTHING I'D HOPED IT WOULD BE: CONDOM-FREE NOOKIE WITH A TOTAL FREAK. AND I LIKE HER, TOO.
GREAT, GREAT. KEEP IT DOWN, THOUGH. DEEDEE COMES HERE OFTEN.
YES, AND EVERYONE HERE IS DEAF.
DARLING BOYS, AND SO PROMPT. DID WE NOT AGREE ON ONE-THIRTY?
ONE, BUT WHY SPLIT HAIRS?
HI, HONEY-BUNS. GIMME SOME SUGAR.
OH LORD.
2:35 P.M.
IF YOU'RE NOT GONNA FINISH--
HELP YOURSELF.
YOU KNOW I DO APPRECIATE APPETITE, RO-BAIR. AND THIS ONE: SUCH APPETITE.
SPEAKING OF: HOW GOES IT WITH YOUR NEW PARAMOUR? DOES THIS ONE HAVE AN EX TO GET BACK TO?
I'M SORRY. I'M SURE SHE'S VERY NICE. JACK TELLS ME SHE'S A FELLOW PORNOGRAPHER.
SHE'S AN ART DIRECTOR.
DARLING, I TEASE. I LOVE THAT YOU'RE SCREWING THE BOSS. IT MUST BE SUBLIME.
NO COMMENT.

SO, ACTUALLY THERE IS AN ULTERIOR MOTIVE TO THIS BRUNCH. DEE AND I WOULD, UH, WE'D LIKE-- UH...
YEAH, WE'D LIKE YOU TO VIDEO US, UM...
ENOUGH FALDERAL. GIVEN YOUR ADULT BONA FIDES, JACKIE AND I WANT YOU TO IMMORTALIZE US IN FLAGRANTE DELICTO.
IRON MAIDEN Killers
I'D LIKE IT NOTED I DIDN'T DANNY THOMAS-STYLE SPIT-TAKE BUKKAKE YOU BOTH WITH HOT COFFEE.
NEITHER OF US IS INTERESTED IN PURSUING ANYTHING DANNY THOMAS-RELATED, THANK YOU. JUST GOOD OLD-FASHIONED CANOODLING.
WE TRIED IT ON A TRIPOD AND IT'S SO STATIC.
I. AM NOT. YOUR MAN.
AND YOU CALL YOURSELF A PORNOGRAPHER.
TUESDAY, AUGUST 15TH, 6:25 P.M.
AWWW. YOU TRIED SO HARD TO NOT DRAW YOUR OWN.
SHIT. MUST BE SUBCONSCIOUS.
IN JAPANESE PORN MANGA THEY SUBSTITUTE PENISES WITH VISUAL METAPHORS LIKE EGGPLANTS AND HOTDOGS. WISH I COULD DO THAT.
I'LL SUBMIT THE INVOICE TOMORROW.
THANKS, "BOSS."
I CAN HEAR THE QUOTES AROUND THAT. CLOSE THE DOOR.
WHY?
tenderloin

SO I CAN CHASE YOU AROUND MY DESK.
AND THEN CATCH YOU. AND THEN DO STUFF.
THERE ARE PEOPLE HERE.
PFF SKELETON CREW ON THIS FLOOR. THEY KEEP US ISOLATED FROM THE BEAVER MAGS.
I DUNNO...
C'MON. I'VE HAD A SUPER SHITTY DAY AND YOU ALREADY SAID YOU CAN'T MAKE A NIGHT OF IT.
THE PRIX AWAIT.
THAT ISN'T CUTE ANY MORE. STUPID NAME FOR A STUPID COMIC BOOK. WHY THEY THOUGHT THAT WAS FUNNY OR COOL--
OKAY, OKAY. BAD ENOUGH I DON'T FEEL GOOD ABOUT ANYTHING I DO FOR A LIVING.
WELL, THAT'S ENOUGH SEXY PILLOW TALK. I KNOW I'M READY FOR ACTION.
UHHHH... I DUNNO, IT'S JUST--
COME ON, ROB. THIS IS CLASSIC PORN SCENARIO: LADY BOSS, SUBORDINATE STUD...
IF YOU DON'T I'M GONNA FEEL BAD ABOUT MYSELF AND GO BE PATHETIC AND EAT ICE CREAM TONIGHT OR SOME WOMANY SHIT.
WHEN YOU PUT IT THAT WAY.

TOO MUCH DICK. THINK MANGA CENSORING. OH GOD: WORSE. DEMONIC. FOCUS ON SHEILA. BUT WHAT IF SOMEONE--
WHAT'S GOING ON? YOU'RE LOSING FIRMNESS. THIS IS TERRIBLE FOR MY SELF-ESTEEM.
YEAH, BECAUSE FUCKING WITH A SOFT-ON IS A REAL EGO-BOOST FOR ME.
IT'S ALL THESE PICTURES EVERYWHERE. A HUNG JURY TOTALLY JUDGING ME.
PLUS, WE'RE IN YOUR OFFICE DURING OFFICE HOURS!
tenderloin
I'M SORRY. I PUT TOO MUCH PRESSURE ON YOU. I JUST WANTED TO DO IT. PLUS, I WAS KINDA HOPING SOMEONE WOULD WALK IN.
WHAT?!? WHY?
SO I'D GET CANNED AND GET SEVERANCE. IMAGINE THE HYPOCRISY OF FIRING ME FOR FUCKING AT A PORN PUBLISHERS.
AND THEY WOULD. EVEN THOUGH AT LEAST THREE OF THE BIGWIGS HAVE TRYSTS IN THEIR OFFICES. REGULARLY.
BUT THEY'RE MEN.
THIS IS THE SECOND TIME IN MY WHOLE LIFE I COULDN'T KEEP IT UP. I DO NOT PERFORM WELL UNDER DURESS.
IT'S KINDA REASSURING THAT ALL THESE DICK PIX WILT YOUR MACARONI.
YEAH. LIKE THE SONG: TOO MUCH PRESSURE. AND DICK. WAY TOO MUCH DICK.
BE GLAD I ADORE DONG. WHATEV'S. YOU OWE ME. SPEAKING OF DICK, LET'S GO BID SAMMY ADIEU.

HOFFMAN INNA HOUSE! YOU COME VISH ME LUCK? I DE NEW SAMMY.
BOOZE MAKES BOLESLAW'S SLAVIC CORE BUBBLE TO THE SURFACE. HILARIOUS.
FINAL DAY, HUH? GLAD I STOPPED BY.
THANKS. UH, NOT SURE BOLESLAW'S GONNA BE ABLE TO KEEP YOU ON THE TEAT.
THERE GOES $1500 A MONTH. FUCK.
I'LL THROW YA SOME BONES AT KIND BUD. BUT THEIR RATES ARE WAY LOWER.
I'VE GOT OUR BOY HERE DRAWING AS MUCH PRONG AS HE CAN HANDLE.
OFF THE TITTY RESERVATION AND ONTO VEINIER VISTAS. AND SOON I'LL HAVE YOU DRAWING FOR DOPERS. DEPLORABLE.
TESLA
ABANDONING US FOR GREENER PASTURES EH, TESLA? GREENER? GET IT?
JUST GOT TIRED OF WEARING A TIE TO WORK, D'ANGE.
THERE THEY'LL MAKE YOU WEAR TIE--
--DYE. TIE-DYE. GET IT? GOOD LUCK WITH THE FREAKS AND HIPPIES.
tenderloin
UH, D'ANGE, THIS IS ROB HOFFMAN. ROB, THIS IS D'ANGELO GANDER.
I DIDN'T KNOW THERE WAS AN ACTUAL--
I ENJOY YOUR CARTOONS. IF YOU'LL EXCUSE ME.
(NO DOUBT OFF TO FUCK SOME CHIPPY. IN HIS OFFICE.)
AT LEAST HE LIKES MY--
(ALL MEN'S MAG HONCHOS LIKE CARTOONS. HEF. THE GOOCH. GANDER. CARTOONS ARE THEIR LEVEL.)
OUCH.
tenderloin

SORRY. HE JUST--
(I LET HIM FUCK ME ONCE. IN HIS OFFICE. UGH, GROSS. ANYWAY, I'LL KEEP LOADING YOU DOWN WITH DICK JOBS. MILK THIS PLACE FOR--)
WAIT, YOU--
ELEVATOR'S HERE. SEEYA LATER, HOFFMAN.
WAIT, WHAT THE FUCK? OW. OW.
PACO
STAR MAINTENANCE
SHEILA FUCKED HER BOSS. PRETTY SURE SYLV WAS FUCKING HERS. BUT I BOTCH A GIFT-WRAPPED SKINEMAX SCENARIO WITH A FLOPPY JOHNSON.
CHRIST, THIS HEAT. UP THERE WITH SHEILA, SOFTNESS. DOWN HERE IT'S NOTHING BUT SWEATY, GLISTENING, CLEAVAGE AND I CAN FEEL--
NO. DON'T THINK ABOUT THE HOT GIRLIES. IMAGINE POST-APOCALYPTIC RUINS.
THAT'S IT. WHAT DID MAD MAX NOT HAVE ON THE BRAIN? SEX. WAIT, WEZ DID. SO...
MUTANT WORLD. CORBEN. YEAH.
ME NO THINK THIS FANTASY WORK FOR YOU.
Tenderloin England

ME LIBIDO-KILLER, BUT CORBEN WRONG CHOICE TO SUPERIMPOSE OVER REALITY. MAKE SEXY GIRL EVEN MORE SEXIER.
UGH, YOU ARE CORRECT.
OKAY, SO MAYBE NOT CORBEN. BUT JESUS, THE GIRLS ARE OUT IN FULL FORCE. THINK ART. BEAUTY. THE ETHEREAL.
MOEBIUS! YOUR IDOL!
tenderloin
THE AIRTIGHT GARAGE. ÆDENA. HIS ARE ABOUT THE ONLY FANTASTICAL WORLDS I'VE EVER TRULY WANTED TO LIVE IN.
BUT HIS WOMEN ARE SUPER HOT, TOO-- URGH!
GODDAMMIT. I WAS RUINED FROM AN EARLY AGE. FIRST TIME I SAW BOOBS IT WAS ALL OVER FOR ME. GOD DAMN IT.

THIS IS MORE MY SPEED. GOES WITH THE TEMPERATURE.
FOR AN **ATHEIST** I SPEND AN AWFUL LOT OF TIME THINKING ABOUT **HELL**.
I **HAVE** A SEX LIFE, *RECENT FLOPPINESS NOTWITHSTANDING*. SHEILA IS **AWESOME**. NOT JUST SEXUALLY, EITHER.
SO WHY CAN'T I SNAP OUT OF IT?
BECAUSE EVEN THOUGH SHEILA IS A GOOD FIT, ONE **DEMONESS** KEEPS **HAUNTING ME**. RIDICULOUS.
THAT'S **RIGHT**, BABY. ***AND I WON'T STOP.***

FOCUS ON THE OTHER SWEATY, GLISTENING DEMONESSES OF SUMMER. BETTER YET, DON'T.
FALLBACK TO ZOMBIES. ROTTING. SMELLY. VILE. THAT SHOULD BANISH SEXUAL THOUGHTS.
OKAY, YOU'RE A SURVIVOR SURROUNDED BY-- NO WAIT--
YOU ARE A ZOMBIE. ONE OF THE HORDE OF GHOULS THAT EXIST ONLY TO DEVOUR WARM HUMAN FLESH. TO CRAM THEIR GULLETS WITH HOT, WET--
OH FOR FUCK'S SAKE. REALLY?
RIGOR MORTIS IN MY "ACTION ZONE." UNBELIEVABLE.

THURSDAY, AUGUST 17TH, 9:30 P.M.
OH GOD, YOU'RE DRESSED AS DEPUTY DEEDEE.
IT'S CALLED ROLE-PLAYING, DEAREST. JACK ALWAYS WANTED--
TO SULLY MY CHILDHOOD MEMORIES?
SIGH LET'S JUST DO THIS.
SO, DO YOU KNOW HOW TO OPERATE THAT?
IT'S A CAMERA. I CAN FIGURE IT OUT.
IT WILL HELP MY PERFORMANCE IF YOU GIVE NOTES.
I'M HERE TO DOCUMENT, NOT DIRECT. CONSIDER THIS A LONG-FORM -- OR SHORT-FORM -- IMPROVISATION.
SHORT-FORM? JEEZ.
DISTURBED
I NEED YOU TO AT LEAST SAY "ACTION."
FINE.
ACTION.
DISTURBED
SO THAT'S WHAT IT LOOKS LIKE FUCKING DEEDEE. I FEEL LIKE I'M HAVING AN OUT-OF-BODY EXPERIENCE. ONLY BALDER AND HAIRIER.
APOCALYPSE? BONER. HELL? BONER. ZOMBIES? BONER.
THIS?
I FEEL NOTHING.
NO, NOT NOTHING EXACTLY...

HE'S PUKING. THAT'S GREAT FOR MY SELF-ESTEEM.
OH HUSH. ROB? ROB, HONEY, ARE YOU ALL RIGHT? WHEN MY SON USED TO GET AN UPSET TUMMY--
YOU HAVE A SON?
ABOUT YOUR AGE. ANYWAY, ROB, DEAR--
--NEVER EAT STREET MEAT. NEVER. MY GOD.
I AM SO SORRY.
COULDA BEEN WORSE. COULDA HAPPENED THIRTY SECONDS EARLIER. THAT WOULD'VE BEEN A MONEY-SHOT ONLY A GERMAN COULD ENJOY.
THAT WAS A MISTAKE. THEY RUINED RANGER RIVERS FOR ME FOREVER. I RUINED BEING VIDEOED FOR THEM. GUESS WE'RE EVEN.
BUT I'VE FINALLY LEARNED WHAT DOESN'T GET ME GOING: SEEING JACK DOING IT.
IS IT BECAUSE IT WAS JACK? OR JUST BEING THAT CLOSE? CLOSE ENOUGH TO SMELL--
HOOOAARRK

SATURDAY, AUGUST 19TH, NOONISH.
--ADD PUBLIC VOMITING TO YOUR RECENT MILESTONES IN DISGRACEFUL PUBLIC BEHAVIOR.
BRONUS, COMMANDMENT *NUMERO UNO*: **NO STREET FOOD**.
I'M **AMAZED** YOU'RE EATING **DINER** FOOD, SWIRL. IN **QUEENS**, NO LESS.
S'CUZ I **LURVS** MY HOMIES I'M WILLING TO SLUM. CUZ I BE **HATIN'** THE **O.B.s**.
HUH?
ONE WAY
STOP
TRAFFIC
TOWER DINER
TOWER
TOWER
OUTER BOROUGHS. TOO MUCH **SKY** HERE. MOSTA MANHATTAN IS COMFORTINGLY **FREE** OF **SKY**.
NOT EXACTLY MONTANA HERE, BUT I KINDA KNOW WHAT MATT MEANS.
THANK YOU, KOBS. SO WHATTAYA **DO** OUT HERE IN REGAL PARK?
REGO.
UCCH. WHATEV'S.
THIS IS A NABE OF QUIET, MEDITATIVE, UH... *HMMM*.
SO, I'M **SEEING** SOMEONE.
FOR **REALSIES?** REGAL PARK **IS** FOR LOVERS. THAT WHAT MY BUDDIES ARE? **LUVVAHS?** WHERE **MINE** AT?
I THOUGHT YOU WERE SEEING THAT BARISTA.
AND THE ONE FROM THE **GYM**, LEST WE FORGET.
THEN WHAT ARE **YOU CARPING** ABOUT? "WHERE **MINE** AT," LEST WE FORGET.
I FORGOT. *TRANSITORY JEALOUSHEIMER'S*. BUT MINE ARE JUST **PHYSICAL**. I WANNA **CONNECT**.
REALLY?
NAH. NOT **NOW**, ANYWAY.

3:42 P.M.
MAN, YOU ARE CRANKING OUT THE CRANK FOR BOY TOY. IF I DIDN'T KNOW BETTER...
YOU DID ALRIGHT WITH THIS CRIB. I'M KINDA THINKIN' I MAY GO SOLO.
REALLY? WOULD YOU LEAVE THE NABE?
NOTHING DEFINITE. I LIKE LIVING WITH THOSE GUYS. AND IT'S CHEAP. BUT NOW THAT I'M SEEING MARY--
I WAS SO GENEROUS GIVING YOU THIS FIGURE. IT'S WORTH A LOT. I HOPE YOU CHERISH IT.
YEAH, WE WEREN'T TALKING ABOUT ANYTHING, ANYWAY.
I LOVE HOW MY BUDDING LOVE LIFE ISN'T AS COMPELLING AS A CARTOON RAT.
A CARTOON MOUSE. DAKIN. VERY RARE. I HAD THIS AND GAVE IT TO KOBS.
YOU WANT IT BACK? IF YOU WANT IT BACK, JUST--
NO, NO. JUST SAYING--
YEAH. HEY, I GOTTA GO GET READY.
DOUSING YOUR SCROTE IN DRAKKAR NOIR?
I NEED TO SHAVE. I--
WHY AM I EXPLAINING TO YOU?
I'M SEEING MY GIRL TONIGHT, TOO.

4:15 P.M.
--FEEL WEIRD LEAVING YOU GUYS IN THE LURCH, BUT--
DON'T SAY ANOTHER WORD. *MAZEL TOV.* IT'S A **GREAT** OPPORTUNITY.
LOS ANGELES, HUH? *WOW.* **MEN'S MAGS** TO **BASIC CABLE**. SOMEONE FINALLY SCENTED YOU HAVE TALENT.
NUH-UH. I DON'T LIKE IT.
I DON'T LIKE YOU LEAVING.
I **GOTTA**. IT'LL BE **GREAT. GREAT JOB. GREAT PEOPLE**. COME VISIT.
I HATE L.A.
S'MATTER: *TOO MUCH SKY?*
HUH?
CALLBACK. NEVER MIND. IT'S AWESOME, BRI. *WE'LL* ***MISS*** *YOU LIKE* ***CRAZY.***
NYU
5:25 P.M.
MATT'S BRIAN AND STAN'S PROBLEM NOW.
WONDER IF STAN'S GONNA WANNA KEEP THE PLACE WITH JUST THE TWO OF US.
YOU WERE JUST SAYING--
I **KNOW**. BUT THAT WAS ***THEN***. S'GONNA BE **WEIRD** WITH BRIAN GONE. TOO BAD YOU GOT YOUR OWN PLACE.
I NEED MY OWN SPACE.
Subway
SO, THIS IS YOUR LOOK FOR MS. MYSTERY.
SHE LIKES ME SCRUFFY.
SO THAT'S ***ONE*** THING I KNOW ABOUT HER.
LOOK: SHE ***ASKED*** ME TO KEEP **MUM** BECAUSE SHE WORKS WITH PEOPLE WE BOTH KNOW AND--
THAT'S FINE, I UNDERST--
IT'S **SHEILA**. FROM ***BOY TOY.***
AH. ***NOW*** IT ALL MAKES SENSE.

--NOT WANTING KIDS WAS THE CLEAREST REASON, BUT IT HAD GOTTEN BAD. SHE WAS VERY MANIPULATIVE. PLAYED MIND GAMES...
AND WAS FUCKING HER BOSS. NOW I KNOW WHY YOU PRUNED UP WHEN I MENTIONED BONING GANDER.
PRETTY SURE THAT WOULDN'T'VE MADE ME HAPPY, REGARDLESS.
ONE WAY
W 69 ST
RESTAURANT
West Side RESTAURANT
West Side RESTAURANT
West Side RESTAURANT
FREE DELIVERY
YOU TALK ABOUT YOUR EX A LOT.
BUT--
YOU ASKED. I WASN'T EVEN GOING TO--
JUST YANKIN' YER CRANK. YA MADE ME FEEL A FRISSON OF GUILT ABOUT GANDER. HADDA DEFLECT.
SPEAKING OF: GIMME, GIMME, GIMME.
THE PEN IS MIGHTIER THAN THE SWORD. PEN + IS = PENIS. TRITE. SORRY. ADDLED BY THE MIGHTY WANG YOU DRAW.
YOU COULDN'T POSSIBLY MAKE ME FEEL LIKE A BIGGER WHORE.
I COULD TRY.
FEEL LIKE A WHORE NOW, HOFFMAN?
NO, MA'AM.
I MUST BE DOING SOMETHING WRONG.
OH, NO YOU AREN'T. NOT EVEN SLIGHTLY.

THAT WAS **AWESOME**. AND YOU MANAGED **NOT** TO GLAZE MY LINENS.
KIDDING. DO NOT CARE.
I GOTTA SAY, I BEEN KIND OF A **MOPE** OF LATE, BUT I'M FEELING REALLY LUCKY. GOOD FRIENDS. NICE PLACE TO LIVE. WORKING REGULAR. **GREAT GIRLFR--**
SO, THIS **EX** OF YOURS--
REALLY? I'M STILL **INSIDE** YOU. BAD ENOUGH MY EX **PLAGUES** MY SLEEP.
ABOUT THAT... I GOT A LOT SWIRLING AROUND IN **MY** HEAD, TOO.
THERE'S JUST NO EASY WAY TO **SAY** THIS...
WAIT. YOU GOTTA BE **KIDDING** ME. I AM **LITERALLY STILL IN YOU.**
IT'S JUST...
OH NO, NO, NO, NO, NO.
WE NEED TO TALK.
AND I'M OUT.

BONUS SECTION

A selection of covers, sketches and pinups.

This page: cover for
Minimum Wage #1

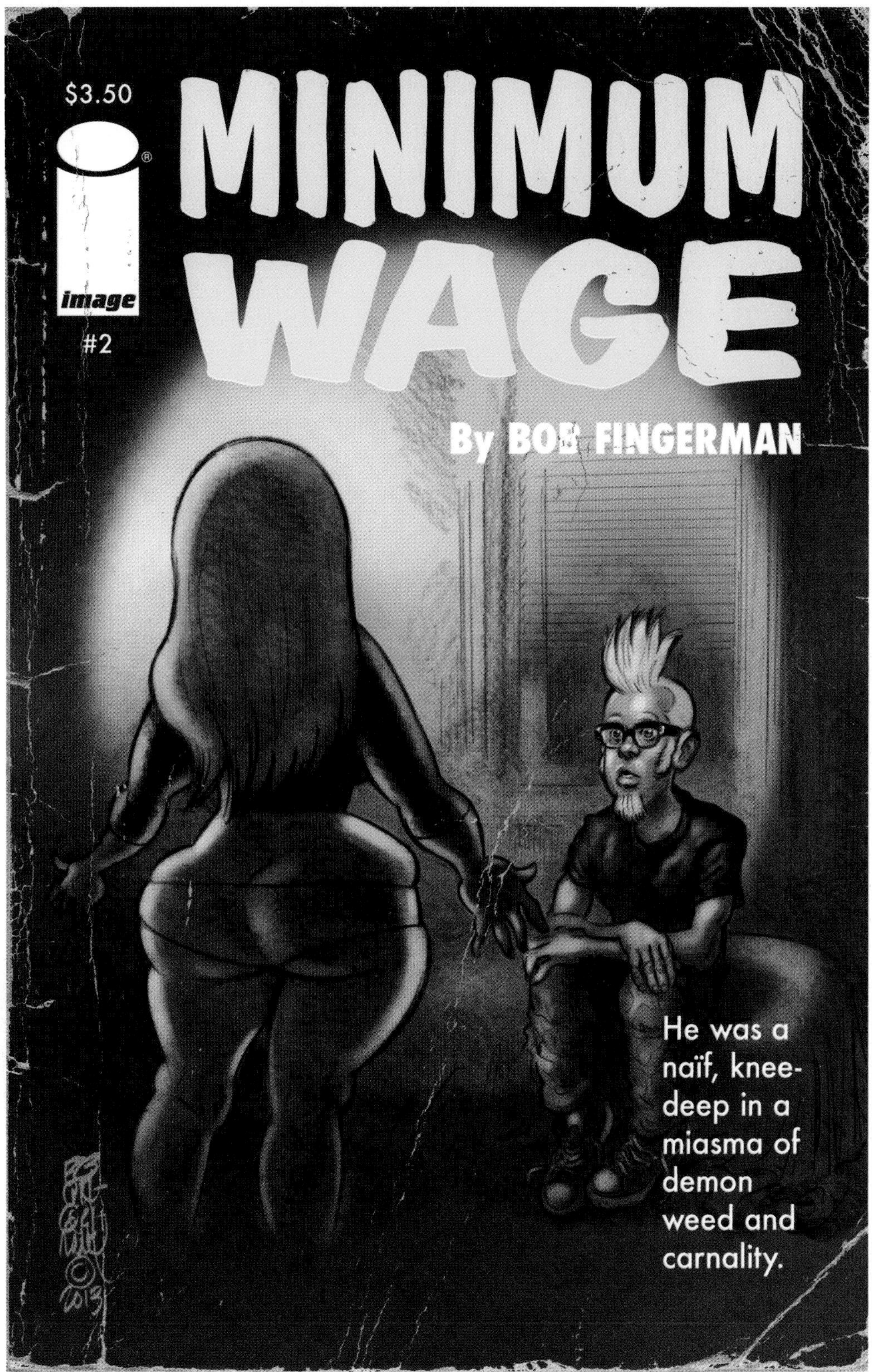

When the idea hit me to do the cover to #2 in the style of a sleazy '60s-vintage drugstore adult paperback I knew I wanted it to look authentically aged and abused. To provide the authentic cracks I scanned the opposite end of the spectrum: that paragon of innocence, a vintage ***Peanuts*** paperback. Yin and yang. Thanks, Fawcett Crest! I also muddied up the art, so opposite is the art, presented for the first time in its pristine glory.

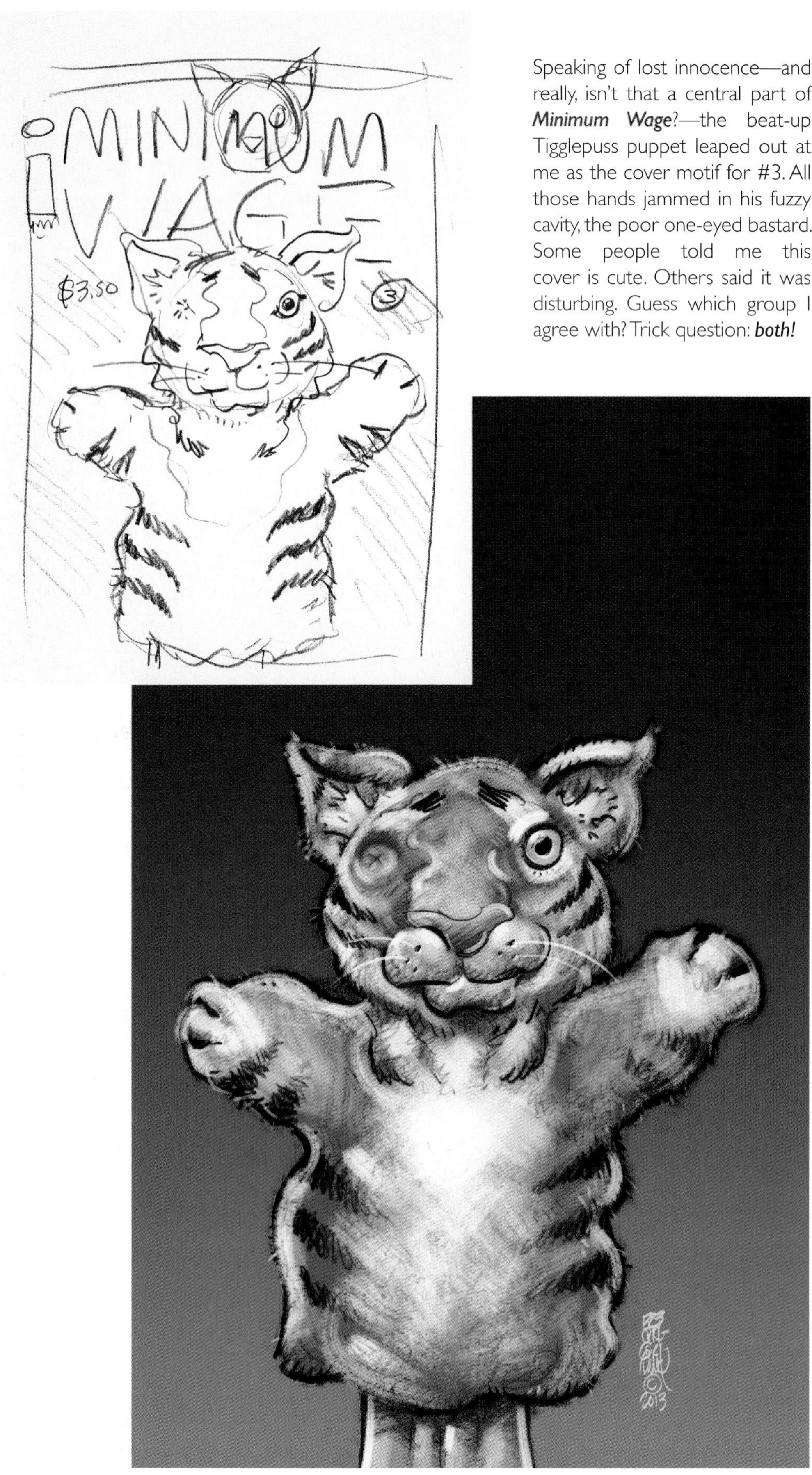

Speaking of lost innocence—and really, isn't that a central part of ***Minimum Wage***?—the beat-up Tigglepuss puppet leaped out at me as the cover motif for #3. All those hands jammed in his fuzzy cavity, the poor one-eyed bastard. Some people told me this cover is cute. Others said it was disturbing. Guess which group I agree with? Trick question: ***both!***

There were a dicey few moments when I worried this cover for #4 might not pass muster as acceptable for display. Fortunately, it got the go-ahead, as I had no other image in mind that I felt accurately conveyed the theme of this chapter.

The initial idea I had for the cover for the first all-new issue in 15 years was Rob surrounded by a sea of women, but the more I thought about it the more I realized I wanted the readers—especially the original ones—to know from the get-go that all was not well in Rob's life. So, I tabled that idea until #5, by which time Rob's status as a singleton was well established. I'm glad I did. I'm also glad you can now see the girls that were obscured by the logo.

This page: cover for *Minimum Wage* #6

©
2014

SKETCHBOOK

Trying to figure out how to draw Rob and the gang wasn't as easy as I thought it would be. I didn't want to even attempt to draw the way I used to. That felt wrong. I like moving forwards, not backwards. So redesigns for all were in order. The first stabs at Rob, in particular, were too embarrassing, so here are some second and third stabs.

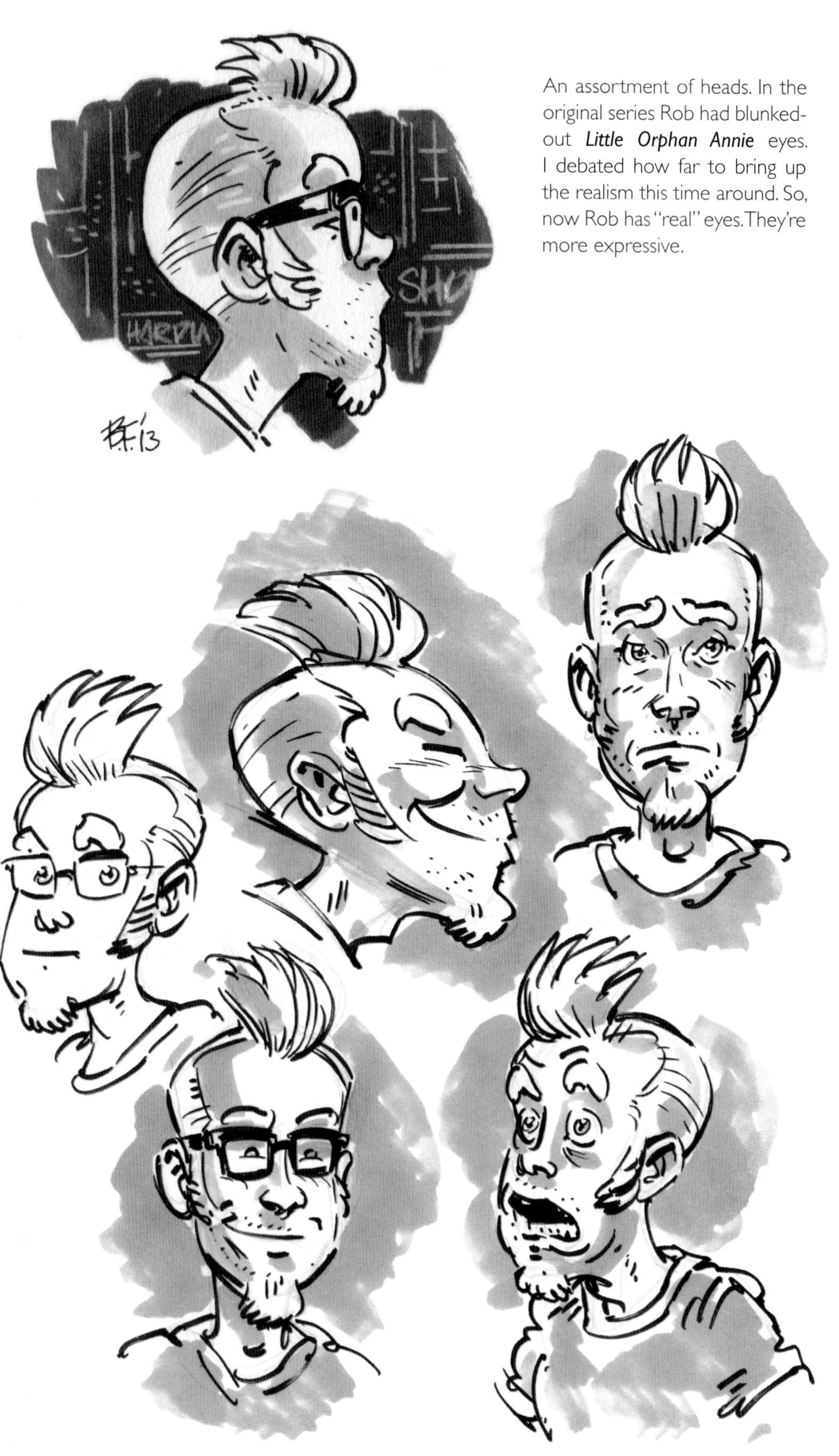

An assortment of heads. In the original series Rob had blunked-out ***Little Orphan Annie*** eyes. I debated how far to bring up the realism this time around. So, now Rob has "real" eyes. They're more expressive.

Brian, in the original run, wore his hair in a ponytail and was much thinner. The friend upon whom Brian was based had weight that over the years fluctuated quite a bit. Tragically, he passed away in January of 2014, right before the new series debuted, which is the reason I chose to have him relocate to Los Angeles (which the real one did, actually). Brian deserves a happy life on the Left Coast. Maybe someday, if I'm able, I will bring his jocularity back to the pages of **MW.**

Designing May, Rob's first post-Sylvia hookup, was a challenge. Note her extremely corny last name, which I wisely discarded. At first I thought Jack would remain pretty much the same, but I scrapped his sharper features, as seen here, in favor of the rounder ones in the pages of the story. Not sure it was the right choice, but I've committed. Sorry, Jack! May proved harder to design than any previous character to date. In the end, though, I really like the drawings on the next page.

B.F. '13
SHE IS DEFINITELY
A DANSKIN TYPE.
B.F. '13
BINGO!!!
6.25.2013

GUEST GALLERY

Gregory Benton's wordless graphic novel ***B+F*** was awarded The Museum of Comic and Cartoon Art's inaugural Award of Excellence at MoCCAFest 2013. In 2014 ***B+F*** was accepted into the Society of Illustrators first Comic and Cartoon Art Annual. The book is available through Adhouse Books (USA), Editions çà et là (France) or wherever fine comix are sold.

J. Bone is a Canadian comic book artist/writer known for his work on ***SAVIORS*** for Image, ***Rocketeer: Hollywood Horror*** for IDW, and as the inker on the Eisner Award-winning one-shot ***Batman/The Spirit***.

Farel Dalrymple made ***The Wrenchies,*** (First Second Books), ***Delusional*** (Adhouse), ***IT WILL ALL HURT*** (Studygroup Comics), ***Omega the Unknown*** (Marvel) with author Jonathan Lethem, and ***Pop Gun War: Gift***.

Joe Dator is a gregarious and debonair bon vivant whose cartoons appears regularly in ***The New Yorker***. He can be seen gregariously and debonairily bon vivanting all over New York City. Bob is his good friend. And so is coffee. www.joedator.com

Joe Flood is a cartoonist and illustrator, whose work includes the graphic novels, ***Hellycity*** and ***Orcs; Forged for War.*** His latest, ***The Cute Girl Network***, written by Greg Means and MK Reed was published by First Second Books. Joe recently completed two issues for a comic book version of the NBC sitcom ***Saved by the Bell.***

Brandon Graham is the creator of comics and graphic novels such as ***King City***, ***Multiple Warheads*** and more. He is also writer of ***Prophet***, the return of a 1990s series, with a rotating roster of artists including Farel Dalrymple and himself.

Danny Hellman has been making art for publication since 1988, and has worked for a wide variety of clients, including ***Time***, ***Newsweek Sports Illustrated***, ***Fortune***, ***Forbes***, ***The Wall Street Journal***, ***Village Voice***, ***New York Press***, ***Screw***, and countless others. Hellman lives in Brooklyn, NY with his wife and daughter.

Douglas Holgate has illustrated comics for Image, Dynamite, Abrams and Random House. He's currently working on the self-published series ***Maralinga*** and an all ages graphic novel ***Clem Hetherington and the Ironwood Race*** both co-created with writer Jen Breach. He lives in Melbourne, Australia.

Gideon Kendall lives in Brooklyn with his wife and fellow artist Julie Peppito and their son Milo. When not making pictures he is usually cooking, writing songs or playing ultimate frisbee. His work can be seen at gideonkendall.com and his graphic novel ***WHATZIT*** is available at WHATZITCOMIC.com.

Scott Kester is an art director and concept artist from Gearbox Software who has contributed to ***Borderlands 1*** and ***2***, and the upcoming game ***Battleborn***.

Kristen McCabe is an artist from Missouri. She loves drawing funny looking people in different shapes and sizes. Check out shmisten.tumblr.com for more of her art.

Carla Speed McNeil reads a lot of pop science and then gets it all wrong, which is why she writes fiction. Writer and artist of long-running science fiction series ***Finder***, now published by Dark Horse.

Maria Schneider is a former associate editor of ***The Onion,*** cartoonist, and comedy day laborer. She is the author of ***The Onion Presents: A Book Of Jean's Own!*** (St. Martin's Griffin), writing as columnist Jean Teasdale. Depending on when you read this, she lives in Jersey City, NJ or Poughkeepsie, NY.

Bill Sienkiewicz Bill Sienkiewicz is known for the graphic novels ***Elektra: Assassin*** (writen by Frank Miller) and ***Stray Toasters***. His non-comics work includes art for films such as ***The Dark Knight***, ***Unforgiven*** and ***The Green Mile***; cover art for videogames, CDs, book covers and magazine illustrations. He also designed multimedia stage productions for Roger Waters' 2006 Dark Side of the Moon Tour.

Mark Stafford draws stuff so you don't have to. He 's the semi-permanent cartoonist-in-residence at the Cartoon Museum in London, and co-created the graphic novels ***Cherubs!*** (with Bryan Talbot) and ***The Man Who Laughs*** (with David Hine) check out www.hocus-baloney.com.

Art by **Gregory Benton**

Art by **J. Bone**

Art by **Farel Dalrymple**

Art by **Joe Dator**

Art by **Joe Flood**

Art by **Brandon Graham**

Art by **Danny Hellman**

Art by **Douglas Holgate**

Art by **Gideon Kendall**

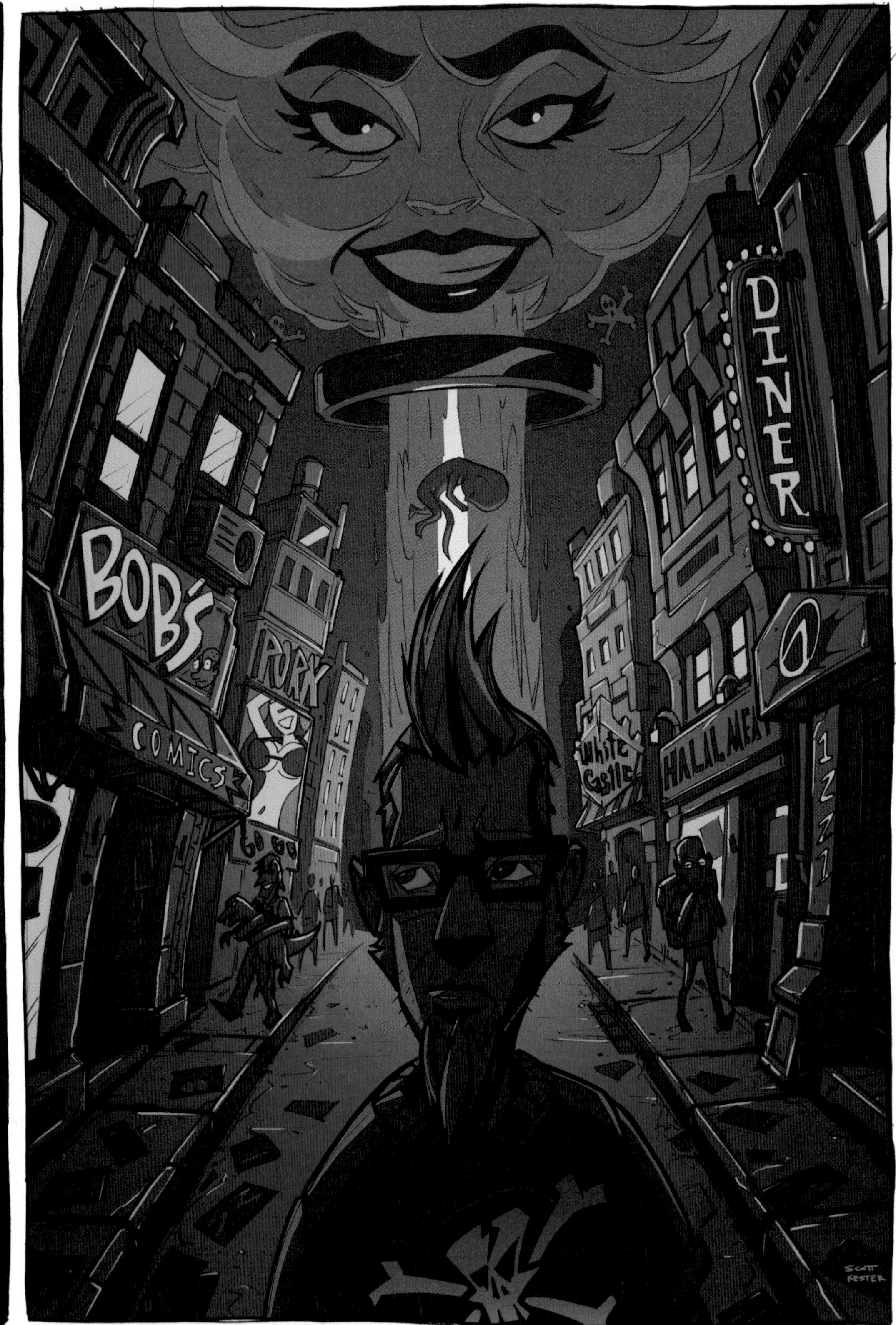
BOB'S
COMICS
PORK
DINER
White Castle
SCOTT KESTER

Art by **Kristen McCabe**

Art by **Carla Speed McNeil**

Art by **Maria Schneider**

Art by **Bill Sienkiewicz**

Art by **Mark Stafford**

Bob Fingerman is best known as the creator of the groundbreaking comic ***Minimum Wage***. "***Minimum Wage***...really showed me what comics could be and has informed my take on writing comics in truly significant ways" says Robert Kirkman, creator of ***The Walking Dead***. Fingerman's career has been marked by a restless creativity that has taken him from illustration to cartooning to graphic novels to prose novels.

A Queens native and only child, Fingerman was one of those kids other kids called "a good drawer." His childhood art heroes were "the usual gang of idiots" at ***MAD***, especially Wally Wood, Sergio Aragonés, Al Jaffee and Don Martin, as well as Charles Schulz and Walt Kelly. Junior high school was rough, but he found a more receptive environment at the High School of Art & Design, taking inspiration from Moebius, Richard Corben, Enki Bilal, R. Crumb, ***Heavy Metal*** magazine, and underground comix.

Fingerman attended New York's School of Visual Arts, where he studied with Will Eisner and Harvey Kurtzman. There, Kurtzman recruited him to work on the young readers anthology ***NUTS!*** Following SVA, Fingerman took on an array of freelance gigs for ***Cracked***, ***Screw***, ***Penthouse Hot Talk***, ***Heavy Metal***, ***National Lampoon***, ***High Times***, ***The Village Voice***, and so on.

Refocusing his efforts almost exclusively on comics, he worked on ***The Teenage Mutant Ninja Turtles*** and several adult comics. He also created covers and short stories for Dark Horse Comics and DC Comics' Vertigo imprint.

In 1993 Fingerman published his first graphic novel, ***White Like She***. He drew the graphic novel in a strict photo-reference style. As a 30th birthday present to himself, he decided to create a comic truer to his own style and vision: the semi-autobiographical series ***Minimum Wage***.

His affection for comics rekindled, Fingerman produced a series of graphic novels: ***Recess Pieces***, ***Connective Tissue*** and ***From the Ashes***, a "speculative memoir" featuring Bob and his wife Michele in post-apocalyptic New York.

Fingerman also began working in prose. His darkly humorous vampire novel, ***Bottomfeeder***, was published in 2006. His second novel, ***Pariah***, envisions a zombie apocalypse set in New York City. "I wanted to alternate between graphic novels and prose novels," he explains. "I always wanted to do both. Ideally, I will. But for now doing comics is keeping me plenty busy and plenty happy."

—Laura Brown, author of ***How to Write Anything***